Into The Valley

Richard Jobson

Into The Valley

Richard Jobson

WYMER
PUBLISHING
Bedford, England

First published in Great Britain in 2020
by Wymer Publishing
www.wymerpublishing.co.uk
Tel: 01234 326691
Wymer Publishing is a trading name of Wymer (UK) Ltd

Copyright © 2022 Wymer Publishing.

ISBN: 978-1-912782-94-9

The Author hereby asserts his rights to be identified
as the author of this work in accordance with sections
77 to 78 of the Copyright, Designs & Patents Act 1988.

All rights reserved. No part of this publication may be
reproduced or transmitted in any form or by any means,
electronic or mechanical, including photocopying, or any
information storage and retrieval system, without written
permission from the publisher.

This publication is sold subject to the condition that it shall not,
by way of trade or otherwise, be lent, re-sold, hired out or
otherwise circulated without the publishers prior consent in any
form of binding or cover other than that in which it is published
and without a similar condition including this condition
being imposed on the subsequent purchaser.

Every effort has been made to trace the copyright holders of the
photographs in this book but some were unreachable. We would
be grateful if the photographers concerned would contact us.

Typeset by Andy Bishop / 1016 Sarpsborg.
Printed by CMP, Dorset, England

A catalogue record for this book is available from the British Library.

Cover design by 1016 Sarpsborg.
Front cover photo © Perry Ogden.
Back cover photo courtesy Richard Jobson.

CONTENTS

Preface	1
Chapter One	3
Chapter Two	7
Chapter Three	11
Chapter Four	15
Chapter Five	19
Chapter Six	23
Chapter Seven	29
Chapter Eight	33
Chapter Nine	39
Chapter Ten	45
Chapter Eleven	53
Chapter Twelve	59
Chapter Thirteen	65
Chapter Fourteen	71
Chapter Fifteen	77
Chapter Sixteen	85
Chapter Seventeen	91
Chapter Eighteen	99
Chapter Nineteen	111
Chapter Twenty	119
Chapter Twenty-One	127
Chapter Twenty-Two	137
Chapter Twenty-Three	145
Chapter Twenty-Four	153
Chapter Twenty-Five	159
Chapter Twenty-Six	167
Chapter Twenty-Seven	173
Chapter Twenty-Eight	177
Chapter Twenty-Nine	185
Chapter Thirty	193
Chapter Thirty-One	201
Epilogue	207
Into The Valley	213

PREFACE

"I'm not a brave man, I've died many times."
- Brave Man, The Skids

As a child I sat in the darkness of the local cinema watching adventure movies dreaming of making an amazing journey myself one day. I had no idea that journey would become a reality so quickly.

And what a journey. If there have been triumphs then there have been as many disappointments. If there has been inspiration and creativity then there has also been tragedy and failure.

Would I have changed anything in retrospect? Yes. Could I have changed anything at the time? Who knows. I didn't write this story in the conventional way of sitting down with pen and paper, or even in front of a keyboard, typing it. Instead I spoke it. I just talked as the thoughts came into my head and that should be evident in the reading style. But it's all my words, straight from within.

This story covers my early life up to the day the Skids adventure came to a close. I've been as honest as I could, never shying away from the fact that I was lost and lonely and sometimes a bit of a wanker.

Into The Valley

CHAPTER ONE

There was a lot of activity in this small council house that we lived in with our mother and father and two brothers at the time. We were travelling to London to meet my grandmother who lived in Earl's Court where she had a newsagent shop. So there was a general sense of excitement. I was told to get out of the way because they were busy packing, so I ran out into the street.

I remember hearing a roar, an unusual sound, something I'd never heard before and it was coming close, really close. We lived at the top of a hill and the sound was coming from the other side of the hill. The roar got louder and suddenly this motorcycle appeared right in front of me and smashed into me. It knocked me to the ground. The motorcyclist was sprawling across the road. His bike was in a terrible state.

I fell down and my head thumped off the ground. I remember the echoes. Everything was in an echo chamber — strange, distant and unreal. I saw people's faces looking down at me. I couldn't make out what they were saying. There seemed to be a combination of concern and anger, but I couldn't work out what they were saying. It was just a very strange experience.

Eventually the words started to filter through the echoes and I could hear my mother speaking to me. She was shouting angrily. It was a big day. Travelling to London in 1964 wasn't easy. It was an epic journey from the rural backwater of Fife in the east of Scotland. And there I was lying on the ground with a tread mark across my face, seemingly having a seizure, the first of many that would come.

This was the beginning of something that would haunt me for the rest of my life. After this accident I would be prone to different types of seizures, mostly from fainting. I could define them as absence seizures. I was misdiagnosed as having a low blood count but in fact it was an early form of epilepsy caused by this accident. All I can remember mostly from that day is the sound and the roar — the impact, and the fury, because the journey to London had been ruined by my stupidity for running out in front of an oncoming vehicle.

The street we lived on was surrounded by hills. It was in a small mining village called Ballingry in central Fife in the east of Scotland. Our home was a two-bedroom council house. My father was a coal miner and my mother at the time worked in the cashmere factory over in Loch Leven in Kinross called Todd & Duncan. In many ways this accident set the tone for my relationship with her for the rest of my life. It always seemed to be on the edge of conflict, always on the edge of some misunderstanding, a complete lack of empathy. It was also the beginning of a journey of being isolated.

The strangeness of this was in many ways the very thing that gave me the opportunity to read books, listen to music and watch movies. I ended up spending an awful lot of time on my own because of that single moment that left me with a condition which has stayed with me to this day.

So out of this horrible negativity came something wonderful in a way. It made me inhabit my own imagination and create a world within a world and really, a lot of the things I've been involved with were born on that particular day.

It wasn't a home with lots of books in the house or music. It was classic working class Scotland. My father worked on different shifts down the mine, which must have been horrific. He never talked about it but it must have been pretty unpleasant. And my mother worked intense hours too. So when they hit the weekend they would find a way to cleanse themselves of the week having worked in really difficult conditions. That was through going to local pubs and working men's clubs and getting themselves into a fairly intoxicated state.

Into The Valley

CHAPTER TWO

Fifeshire in the 1970s was a difficult place. There was a lot of unemployment. There were few jobs for young people coming out of schools and the steady route into becoming a tradesman like your father, maybe in the dockyard in Rosyth, or the coalmines of central Fife and beyond was becoming increasingly difficult. Industrial action was going on all over. Fife was known as a particularly militant place; still is to this day. It was regarded as a hive of communist activity.

My father was quite a reactionary and politically militant character. So when the miners of central Fife would strike he would be right at the forefront of that which made life very difficult of course. We had no idea as young guys, my two brothers and I, what was going on but we knew things were difficult. Indeed things were never that easy in the first place and they became increasingly difficult.

So our home life was fairly austere but beyond where we lived, the actual landscapes were truly remarkable. Beyond the street where we lived were the Benarty Hills. I used to walk up those hills through an area called The Avenue — an avenue of trees, past the ruins of Lochore House where Sir Walter Scott's lover, Miss Jeanie Jobson, had once lived. I don't think there's any relation but who knows?

I'd walk up those dark avenues and then get to a rocky

crevice, climb over and walk over the plateau at the top of the hill which would take quite a few hours and eventually you're on the other side with the magnificent vista of Loch Leven, where certainly in the late spring and summer months I would spend most of my time.

Without having particularly any sense of aesthetic I knew that the area was a special place. The walk to the Loch was a great adventure, living in my own imagination, creating stories, dramas, narratives, spectacular re-enactments of battles from World War II or creating a sense of mystery born from books like *The Famous Five*. But more than likely books I had started reading like Sir Walter Scott's *Ivanhoe* which gave me a daring do sense of adventure.

So that became a really special and important place in my life: The landscape, the air and the water. Having a paperback book in my back pocket as a young kid, getting away from the poverty of my home up into those hills and hanging out at the loch, reading, was very special.

My elder brother, Francis was quite an amazing guy. He had started to introduce me to literature at a very early age, mostly science fiction, but it made a huge mark on me as a young kid. Isaac Asimov, John Wyndham, Brian Aldiss, books that really meant a hell of a lot to me because they have a sense of adventure, a frontier spirit. But of course it wasn't like the Wild West, it was out there in space.

Of course this sense of being wrapped up in narratives and stories, books and the landscape, in many ways highlights the isolation I was going through as a kid. And the sense that something wasn't quite right and hadn't been right since the terrible moment that motorcycle hit me and knocked me into the air, banged my head and suddenly finding myself on a near daily basis prone to fainting fits and very mild seizures..

To try and give myself a sense of community, because

I didn't really get that at home, I spent a lot of time at St Bernard's Church, adjacent to the Catholic school, St Kenneth's in Ballingry that I attended. The school obviously encouraged pupils to be an active member of the church. If you were able to spend time there and work in the church, which I did as a youngster, the local priest, Father Wilson, was fundamentally a good guy. I think he was a socialist more than a priest. He understood the poverty that was prevalent in the area. Social dysfunctionality of a lot of the families was causing tremendous damage to the young children.

So there was a gang of us who used to work in the church and I became an altar boy, but unfortunately the fainting and the unconscious state I constantly found myself in, happened many, many times during his services. It became very frustrating for him because he obviously wanted the people in the mass to listen to him and he wanted their attention. So it didn't really help when there was this young kid who kept on fainting and smashing his head on the beautifully polished wooden floors.

But nonetheless, the Catholic Church definitely in the early years of my life gave me great solace. I enjoyed the stories that were born out of The Bible, and definitely through Father Wilson and the politics of the area we lived in, I had a deeply embedded sense of social injustice and a moral strength came from that.

In later years of course the Catholic Church's reputation has been absolutely destroyed. But I have no recollection of anything like that happening to any of my friends, myself, or family members. The church in our area was a bastion of hope and that's really what you could only ever want from religion or that kind of place. Of course in later years any sense of religion was dropped out of my life but certainly when I needed it, it was there for me. At that point I think I really needed it because my life was complicated. I was about eight or nine years old, and I didn't really catch a sense of the disruptive nature of the poverty that we had lived in and what that was doing to people through alcohol abuse and domestic violence. It's crazy to think back to those times but a lot of the kids were coming to school suffering from malnutrition. In retrospect it's quite shocking but at the time I was almost completely oblivious to the reality of it because I'd created a fantasy world to inhabit that helped me with my poor health condition which was something I had to deal with on a daily basis.

CHAPTER THREE

Close to where we lived, there was an elderly lady called Nan Pride who lived with her mother. She had been in the Army as a cook and now worked in schools, working in the kitchens. My mother occasionally, when she would have days off from the cashmere factory in Kinross, would do lots of small jobs just to try and get enough money to put some food on the table. Mother would work as a cleaner in Nan Pride's house and also helped occasionally to look after Nan's mother when Nan was still working in the kitchens.

I would accompany my mum over to that house. It was a house that seemed very strange — bigger than ours, full of Victorian furniture, quite dark, and it had a quite ominous feel about it. But the one thing I loved about the place is that it was head-to-toe-full of books of every variety. The were lots of religious books — they were deeply Protestant — about various forms of Lutherism and the Bible in many different formats. But there was also the kind of books that I had recently discovered, like Sir Walter Scott and other adventure stories.

I would love going over to this house and sit and read. Occasionally I would read to Nan's elderly mother, who was bed-bound. She had a high Victorian bed, which was quite scary for a little kid. She also had an old-fashioned Victorian commode, which she would actually use, and occasionally, my job was to empty that, so it was a harsh introduction to elderly care.

I had a good relationship with this old lady, so Nan started to invite me over more. I think she already understood that I was having a difficult time with my parents who were drinking too much alcohol and weren't keeping an eye on my health condition that needed some attention, which, of course, was beginning to affect my day-to-day life.

Inviting me over more was a pretty amazing experience because she was an incredible cook. The food was always home-made with extraordinary smells and flavours. She encouraged me to read and read to her mother, which her mother really liked, right up to the moment she died a few years later.

Then Nan started to buy me books, just strange little stories about such things as pioneer children in the Far West of America or Canada. Eventually, she also understood my fascination with science fiction, so started to bring me some science fiction books, although a lot of them were a little bit advanced for me at that time, but I tried to read them anyway. I became a vociferous reader, helped and abated by Nan Pride, who also stabilised my health by encouraging me to eat better foods and have a more stable life.

To all intents and purposes, she adopted me, and I started to spend all my time at her house. At the end of a school day, for example, I wouldn't go home; I'd just go to her place and have some food, do my homework, read, and started to sleep better, so my health started to improve a little bit.

I seemed to be living there full time, she encouraged me to go and see my mum and dad or my brothers, but I just wasn't really interested in seeing them anymore. And even though she was a Protestant, she encouraged me to continue working at the church on a Sunday. She would walk me to the Catholic church, she would then walk across the road into the Protestant church, and afterwards, she would pick me up and take me back to her house again for a pretty amazing Sunday lunch. So I was certainly introduced to a stability and warmth and kindness that, really, I had never seen to that point.

But the biggest thing she did was buy me a little bicycle. This gave me a freedom that I had never had before. Of course, I could go walking up the hills and go swimming in the lochs, but this bike suddenly connected me to the other towns. Because Ballingry was quite remote, and unless you had money to get on a bus, it was quite far away to get to the nearby towns of Lochgelly, Cowdenbeath, or the big one, which was Dunfermline. Or even the place where I was actually born, Kirkcaldy. They were all quite far off, or seemed so to a young boy at least. But I had this bicycle, and it suddenly gave me freedom which in turn gave me the opportunity to do things that I never dreamt that I could do.

I used to, as I say, help Nan with her mother, and then I used to chop the logs to create kindling for the fires and fill all the coal buckets. Nan always rewarded me with a few pennies and that money I saved. I always took myself off on a Saturday morning on my bicycle, first thing, whether it was raining or snowing, I didn't care — to go to this cinema in Lochgelly, where they had a Disney Club which started at 10:30 and went through pretty much until the late afternoon, when they would start the adult films.

And those Disney Club mornings, if you paid your couple of pennies to get in, you could just stay in it for the rest of the day. They were pretty much packed solidly full of kids. The parents dropped them off, pretty well behaved, considering we're all from fairly feral backgrounds. That cinema obviously introduced me to animation, but also Westerns — very basic B-movie science fiction films and of course pop culture film things such as Beatles movies, which were great fun.

So suddenly, this kind of desire for stories and narratives had a new visual form in front of me in this cinema, and it was the most exciting thing I felt at the time. It was just so dramatic — the change it brought to my life. Sitting, watching, it could be a *Tom and Jerry* movie through to a Western with Alan Ladd and then suddenly, you're watching a B-movie sci-fi film that was scary. Then on to something that was just great fun, either a comedy or the Beatles films I loved so much.

The first time I saw *Yellow Submarine* was in this particular cinema. That movie had a combination of everything that I loved, the madness of the animation, the craziness and the fun of the group. They seemed to be a gang without violence, and that's one of the things I understood in later life about being in a band. You're in a gang, but it was not a violent gang.

So that little bicycle, and the kindness of that woman had suddenly stabilised my life in such a way that I was able to explore new avenues through going to the cinema or just cycling through these nearby towns, which had seemed so remote before, but suddenly were within distance. The bike was nothing fabulous, to look at but it became the most important and glorious part of my life.

CHAPTER FOUR

My parent's marriage was occasionally completely insane and violently aggressive. I remember lying in my bed at night listening to them arguing and hearing the sounds of their fighting. The echoes that spun around the room caused me to have mild seizures as I heard them going at each other hammer and tong. And I really mean they were violent towards one another. It was scary stuff.

It transpired that my father had been having an affair. My mother had found out and reacted incredibly violently to the news. It seemed to give her an excuse to drink even more alcohol which she did in an abundance anyway. How she ever held down all the jobs she did I'll never know.

I sometimes had to go and work with her in the fields, picking potatoes in the late summer / early autumn, into the winter and it was really tough. You picked what was called the stent which was a marked distance and the farmer would come up and down the field with his tiller just uprooting the potatoes. Your job was to fill the baskets, then the lorries would come and throw them on. It was backbreaking stuff and it was mostly women who worked there, as their husbands were working in the coalmines. And just to subsidise their income they worked in these pretty tough conditions and a lot of their kids worked with them.

My parents marriage was really on a steady road to a

complete breakdown when they decided to move to a new village to get away from what maybe was the scene of the crime. This was about the same time that I was about to start going up to my high school, St Columbus, which I was very nervous about. I was still having lots of problems with fainting and these seizures which happened at night mostly, but they fed this terrible sense of trepidation and anxiety for a young kid.

I was about 11 or 12 years old. This would be 1971. I was heading up to St Columbus High School in Dunfermline which seemed like a million miles away. Lots of new people from different villages were there; it had a reputation of being a tough place so I was fairly anxious about the whole thing. Then suddenly we moved to a new house.

I spent a bit of time with my father on my own, not much, but occasionally I'd go to the football with him to see Hibernian in Edinburgh. We'd normally go on a Tuesday night when they played in the Fairs Cup and they had quite a fantastic team. I really love football, but I think in my heart even though I'd go and see Hibs my team was Celtic.

It's almost a cultural thing. I was brought up as a Catholic and in the area we were brought up in it was essentially Irish; Celtic Football Club have a huge identity within that culture and you just grow into it. It's not even a matter of choice; that's how it is.

But it was interesting to be with him on my own. He was a quiet guy. A very handsome man and he created an aura, but he obviously was unhappy with his life and it's only in later years it was revealed why he may have been unhappy. His mother lived in London, she had remarried, and she really didn't want to have much to do with him. He had a sister, Isabelle, who was married to an Italian man and she also lived in Fifeshire but in much nicer conditions.

Probably a comfortable lower middle class, a life so much better than his.

Also his mother spent time with them but never spent any time with him or his family. I don't think she approved of my mum who was from a fairly chaotic background. She didn't really know who her father was. It was classic working class, a bit of Irish in there, a bit uproarious and occasionally insane.

My Father's background is actually quite interesting; he's from German ancestry, from a family called the Hulskramers who were from lower Saxony in north- western Germany and from the East Frisian Islands. So if you go back to places like Wilhelmshaven or the East Frisian Islands you can relocate that name, Hulskramer. So he really came from a background which should have given him a really nice step-up in life because he was essentially privileged but he had nothing, he worked down a coalmine from the age of 14 / 15, and he married my lunatic mum. So I think maybe the truth of the matter is that he was disowned.

Into The Valley

CHAPTER FIVE

So I began at this new school, St Columbus in Dunfermline, with a sense of excitement because it was a new page being turned, but again, this nagging sense of not fitting in or being part of the overall thing, like the community of the school or the small cliques and gangs that were created. I still felt very isolated from that.

But one saving grace at this early stage was Francis, who was a really talented artist. He had wanted to go to art school but nobody had approved of that. Nobody encouraged him or helped him and he'd got himself into a little bit of trouble by going off to festivals in England and getting involved with some guys in a drug deal with some Lebanese grass that he sent to somebody in an open book and he got caught. This was during all the IRA bombing at the time and they were suspicious that the package was a bomb, which is how he got caught and he was in big trouble.

At that point in time I shared a room with him. He had painted the room for me with murals from the Marvel Comics which I loved and which he had introduced me to. So Spider-Man, Captain America and the Hulk. I absolutely loved those characters, especially Spider-Man which he created on the door that went up into the ceiling and it was pretty extraordinary. Also he had a record player in there, which was quite a rare thing for somebody from his background to have and his vinyl collection started to grow.

I'd been listening to his music with him and I was still a fairly innocent young kid but suddenly I was listening to Captain Beefheart and Frank Zappa. I was listening to Faust, Can, and the kind of stuff that started to appeal to me more, which was Lou Reed, Iggy Pop, MC5, David Bowie and Leonard Cohen. All of this music was available when he wasn't around so I started to listen to it on my own and really connected with it big time, especially Lou Reed whose lyrics and performance style really captured something special in me.

And of course David Bowie. I've loved David Bowie since I was a ten-year-old kid. I first saw him on *Top of the Pops* and I've never stopped loving him to this day. So this was the kind of music I was listening to which was fairly transgressive and in some ways avant-garde. Not the sort of stuff that my friends — well I wouldn't say friends — but acquaintances I'd met at school were listening to. They were listening to Yes, Genesis, Queen, much more straightforward stuff which I absolutely hated.

And I didn't really know why I hated it but I just knew I hated it, whereas Lou Reed, Iggy Pop and David Bowie as I'm sitting writing this are looking down at me from the photographs I've collected by various rock 'n roll photographers through the years so they're with me every day.

And through the connection between this music, the Marvel Comics, and the science fiction I was reading, I started to think about other things like what my identity was and the way I dressed. I started to dress differently with clothes that I found in second-hand stores so that I would not look the same as everybody else, who at that time was wearing an identikit but I found another way to find out who

I might be.

Unfortunately this all came to an abrupt end when Francis was caught and put in prison for sending on his small amount of drugs. When the police came to the house I knew that hehad stashes of cigarettes hidden in one of the cupboards and that was probably where he was getting his money for buying all of his records, and going to various concerts — he was selling them on the small black market. I managed to hide all of them as these policemen came through the house looking for more drugs. They didn't find any more of course, but they didn't find the cigarettes either.

But it was a real shock to lose probably the biggest influence culturally that I'd ever had. An amazing guy who had been as affected by the dysfunctionality of his home life as I had but, had rebelled in a way that people just didn't understand. He was so different from the macho and traditional type of male from that working- class area.

For example his younger brother and my older brother, John was an amazing football player and was already making strides to becoming a professional although at the time he worked in the dockyard in Rosyth. He was an amazing player and a good guy, but he chose a more traditional route opposed to Francis' more awkward and strange route which inevitably was to lead to his tragic death and it's something I've always had huge problems dealing with.

Into The Valley

CHAPTER SIX

It took a while to fit in at my school. I found making friends more difficult than it should have been and I spent a lot of time on my own which made me look like quite an isolated, solitary figure.

One of the areas that essentially, brought people together was football. Although my health wasn't fantastic I started to excel at being a defender, which is a ridiculous thing because most people always want to become a forward player, where all the glory is. But, I was quite happy in defence. So somehow or other I ended up getting picked for the school team, which was a shock to me and to all around me. But from that moment onwards I felt that I started to be accepted by the people who had normally ignored me. My displays for the school weren't bad I certainly wasn't a great player but I wasn't bad and I could be relied on.

So things started to change because of that. Suddenly, I found myself with the main guys in my year at school, who were all playing for the school team, and I was one of them. Surprise, surprise, I found the gateway into some sense of camaraderie and friendship and togetherness which, up until that point, had completely avoided me. So there was a big change.

Also, coming from that was a sense of how these other guys thought about things like music, clothes and how they considered themselves a great catch for some of the girls from the school, which of course they weren't. The good-looking girls in our school, really, would have nothing to do with feral scumbags like us. They always held their nose up in utter disgust. Essentially, a Catholic school attracted people from both quite wealthy and lowly backgrounds, like myself. So there was definitely a social division in the school and that was more prevalent amongst the female pupils.

Through this new banter and realisation, that I was being accepted through being part of the football team, I started to develop a social life with these new friends. It was interesting to listen to their music, which pretty much followed the pattern along the lines of bands like Genesis, Yes, and Wishbone Ash. All this stuff I really hated, so it was a bit of a shock. Then I started to introduce them to the music I was into. They had never heard of it, the more extreme stuff like Captain Beefheart and Frank Zappa or more transgressive stuff like David Bowie and Roxy Music, and of course Lou Reed. They were quite appalled by all of that.

Meanwhile, my home life had changed yet again because my parents were going through fairly scary times. Their marriage was on the verge of completely crumbling. So they made another move to an outlying area away from the main villages, where we had been brought up, to a rural area in the west of Fife called Saline and it was really remote. It was at the foot of the Ochil Hills, on the border of Clackmannanshire, next to quite wealthy towns such as Dollar, where there were private schools and quite grand hotels, which is not very far from the famous golfing hotel resort, Gleneagles.

Suddenly, I found myself in a completely different situation and really didn't like this new world that I had been thrown into, as my parents tried to navigate a way to save their marriage. Essentially, it was disguised as the home was closer to the new coalmine my father worked in, which was called Solsgirth, just up the road, and which made his life easier.

In many ways we had left a whole life behind in those central Fife mining villages, with their own particular vernacular which only people from that area can ever understand. So suddenly, I was in a different place. The people were absolutely fine but I never really took to the place. It was at that point of time I started to hang out with a guy called Johnny Jameson who was originally from the west of Scotland. He and his mother, and I think his older sister, had moved into Fife when Glasgow was being depopulated from the urban sprawl and poorer areas, and were suddenly in a place called Inverkeithing which is a town next to Rosyth. I started to hang out more and more with him, because we had a similar taste in music. Although, he really did love Genesis and nothing could ever change my views on that band, nothing. But, besides Genesis, we became good friends, both of us were interested in fashion and of course girls. There was a movement towards a certain style at the time. A lot of the guys wore Wrangler Bags and Monkey Boots, a mixture of football clothing: skinhead, suedehead, and boot boy. It was fairly idiotic stuff and didn't look very good.

I actually took a lot of influence from my older brother, John, who was wearing clothes that he was getting from Glasgow from a shop called *Argyle House* in Buchanan Street and a shirt tailoring shop, called **Arthur Black,** in St Enochs Square. These clothes were pretty hip in Glasgow at the time because they were gang related. If you were a member of a specific gang, you would go to either of those shops to have coloured coordinated clothing created for you which identified you with the gang that you were a member of. That started very slowly moving to Fife.

John, was pretty keen on those types of clothes. They were really cool designs that used classic Scottish, and Shetland Isle designs, but taking them into a much more malevolent world.

The clothes from *Arthur Black* were very highly designed shirts and trousers. Very tailored, very aggressive and dynamic in dark blacks and blues with reds, with turned up sleeves. Later on, I was to find out that the amount of buttons you had on the sleeve determined the amount of gang fights you had been in. So this type of clothing started to move through into our world.

At the same time I was listening to more and more music by Lou Reed. The album, *Berlin*, had such an amazing effect on my life. I had no idea at the time that people really hated that album but I truly loved it and it became a massive influence. I remember playing air guitar to the whole album. I indirectly understood that it was a concept album and it was telling a story not unlike reading a piece of fiction. But the music was so engaging and haunting and very moving and it's melancholy spirit touched a nerve with me. It's an album that I loved then and I love today. I still play *Berlin* and I would still suggest it as my favourite album ever made. At the time it was a game changer for me.

That and another Lou Reed album which was a live LP called *Rock 'n' Roll Animal* with these amazing guitar players, Dick Wagner and Steve Hunter doing the most tremendous guitar solo introduction to Lou Reed's entrance onto the stage and it's still incredible to listen to that music even today.

Francis had left the house by then but he had left his

architectural T-square which I used as a guitar. That was my first approach to actually thinking about performing as a member of a band in my own fantasy world as I played along to the mighty Steve Hunter and Dick Wagner and imagine myself as Lou Reed as he strutted on stage as a Rock 'n' Roll Animal.

And of course through the strange story at the heart of *Berlin*, a story of a broken marriage which had such a haunting end to it. In many ways, I guess, that reflected what was happening in my own parent's life because what was going on between my mother and father at the time was pretty dynamic. They were constantly at war and couldn't really find peace in their lives anymore and a lot of that was dictated by alcohol which made my life even more and more difficult.

But, the music kept me alive. *Station To Station* by Bowie, Leonard Cohen, *Hard Nose the Highway* by Van Morrison, Nico's solo album and The New York Dolls. The Sensational Alex Harvey Band, were always there to keep me in my fantasy world which I was now emerging from. That fog of being isolated and feeling incredibly lonely, to suddenly being part of the group, part of what was going on around me. Starting to realise that clothes, music and the books you were reading gave you an identity.

I also always knew I was different from the people around me. I wasn't better I wasn't any worse, I was just different because my life was a little bit more difficult than theirs because of some of the things I had to go through. Especially with these constant mild seizures at night which caused me such distress and made my day very difficult because I'd go to school the next day not having had very much sleep. Compounded that with the aggressive relationship between my mother and father which would go on to the early hours, made it a tough place to be.

That was until I got myself a pair of headphones and suddenly those headphones gave me some respite and it was at that point in time I started to listen to a far away DJ down in London. First on long wave and eventually on medium wave. A guy called John Peel and he'd be playing the most extraordinary music and that music was to change the way I saw the world forever more.

CHAPTER SEVEN

My school started a music club and we had a fairly progressive music teacher, one of the few areas of schooling I was interested in, and he started to take us to concerts.

The first band we went to see was Barclay James Harvest which I really didn't like very much and unlike the rest of the people in my group who were there, who were all sitting back with their eyes closed taking it all in, I was in a state of shock by how awful it was. It just wasn't my kind of music. I was also very aware of how uncool the audience were.

Again this was subconsciously telling me that I didn't really have much in common with these people and that their view of the world, seen and heard through music was completely opposed to how my world was.

I became quite argumentative with my fellow pupils who were members of this music club and they started to strongly dislike me. My views were very forthright about the music that they were listening to which I found bland, disingenuous, self-indulgent, boring, flat and dull, and the people in these bands were like dinosaurs.

They were people who had such a vastly inflated opinion of themselves and this awful music they were making with these rubbish lyrics that had absolutely no poetry about them. I really held my ground on this and started to form a very strong opinion about identity through music at this point in time. I've got to say that the people around me started to get deeply annoyed with me, including my music teachers from the school. But I held onto my beliefs.

As for school generally... I did like English very much and my English teacher introduced me to a lot of great sources and was obsessed with Shakespeare. That's understandable because it's pretty extraordinary stuff; it wasn't a foreign language. It was actually deeply poetic and very rich and the characters were illuminating and tragic and funny.

I also did very well in German. My German teacher was great and I really enjoyed learning the language. German grammar was pretty difficult but I really took to speaking it and it was one of the few classes I attended. It was either music, sports, German, or English, and the rest of it I just really wasn't particularly interested in.

A lot of the other lessons I started to skip and hung out with people from the neighbouring area which was called Abbey View. It was a fairly rundown area and it had a notorious gang from there called the Abbey View Toi. A lot of the gangs in Scotland adopted Chinese names like Toi. The AVT as they were known, were quite a crazy bunch of guys. They were at the local Protestant school for the most part, although some of them were also at my school, St Columbus.

I started to hang out at the shops in Abbey View with these crazy people. They seemed to be interested in good music. They all loved David Bowie and Roxy Music. I had a fairly low opinion of hippies and really didn't like heavy metal or standard rock music very much — something they shared.

They were all a bit older than me but I started to hang out with them, even go to football games. They all supported for some reason, the Edinburgh team Heart of Midlothian who were quite rough with a tough following and the guys from Abbey View seemed to fall into that particular group.

I went with them to a few of the Hearts games which was strange as I was brought up to support Hibernian, the other Edinburgh team. I think there was also a bit of a mild sectarian divide between them, Catholic and Protestant, Hearts being the Protestant team. But most of these Abbey View guys weren't really interested in sectarianism. They were interested in something which was an area that I'd avoided but suddenly there it was right in front me.

Violence seemed to be in the air. All of us had just been submerged into the world of Stanley Kubrick's *Clockwork Orange* where young people were shown on screen in a way that wasn't patronising, and it wasn't boring, and it wasn't about a class division. It was about enigmatic, individualistic, strong-minded and psychotic young people who had a Nihilistic approach to life, which was completely indulgent and extremely dangerous.

So the movie, although you knew the central character, Alex, was bad and what he did was wrong, there was something still exhilarating about his journey in this retelling of a kind of crime and punishment story. Alex and his Droogs were probably the first time that my generation had seen a representation of ourselves on screen that we didn't find boring.

So all this was in the mix at the time. All these strange things going on. Music was changing. There was an edginess that was creeping into the music of Roxy Music and Bowie for example, with his new stuff, *Station to Station*. Whilst in the mainstream, the more traditional bands, were just becoming blander and more boring.

The world that I was interested in suddenly became

more identifiable with a kind of Nihilism which was a potent mixture of watching Kubrick's movie, reading George Orwell, listening to David Bowie, and then being amongst a very violent gang that prosecuted violence in a way that was pretty abhorrent. And I was in the middle of all of that.

I was coming to the end of my period in the school where I just didn't want to stay on. I didn't want to be there anymore. I wanted to go out and find myself as an adult and find my own identity, get away from where my parents lived in this rural area. I wanted to get away from their madness. I wanted to inhabit my own world. My own world was a cacophony of anxiety at that time and I think it was one of the first periods when I started to understand that in some ways this reflected my health condition. That I didn't really think I was going to be around for much longer, so what the hell, let's just enjoy the fuck out of life.

CHAPTER EIGHT

School was coming to an end. The crazy world I had entered of music, fashion, gangs, football, was just this mass of stuff going on that, in many ways, was an excuse or a reason to not look at the reality of my own home life, which was not good. I hated where I lived. My parents were really unhappy with one another and didn't really show much compassion for anybody else in this world. By then my two younger brothers Michael and Brian, were probably suffering what I had been through, with this tension and constant aggression being in the air. So whenever I was there I'd bury my head under the covers, mostly to keep warm because it was so cold — the house was freezing cold — but also to listen to music, and again, listen to John Peel every night.

Peel was like this harbinger of happiness. Somebody who brought joy to your life. He was like a lighthouse that spread — rather than light — spread music, and music I had never heard before, or artists who I had never considered before. People like U-Roy and I-Roy, wonderful reggae artists, or Ivor Cutler the avant-garde poet; Van der Graaf Generator; mixed with a lot of pub R'n'B music coming out of London. The 101ers, Joe Strummer's early band; Nick Lowe's music; Dave Edmunds; Graham Parker & The Rumour; Southside Johnny & The Asbury Jukes. This was all music that was flooding out from this lighthouse of musical sanity that was John Peel.

I didn't listen to much else. The music that was played during the day on Radio One was pretty terrible. The local stations in Scotland were turgid to say the least. And the more grown-up stations like Radio Two, or even Radio Scotland were so middle-class and up themselves that the idea that they'd do anything or play anything interesting was pretty much impossible.

So, Peel was the guiding light that gave you a sense that something was coming. You didn't know what, but you felt something was coming. These behemoths, these dinosaurs, these bands that were so huge and enormous that they had their own private planes as they went on their world tours. It was really grotesque.

Occasionally you would see them on television on shows like *The Old Grey Whistle Test*, which was presented by Bob Harris, who seemed to know his music inside out. But for me the music was quite difficult to relate to. Occasionally there'd be something on there, John Martyn maybe — for example, Peter Hammill — that just gave you a sense that maybe something else was going on in this world that was beyond the horror of these nasty super-groups and old dinosaurs who were so boring.

By this time Francis had become a fully-fledged Hare Krishna monk and I had started to visit him in the Temple in Edinburgh. He understood my frustration of not being very happy at home. Music was beckoning me, and at the same time I was involved with these quite violent people, and he said to me that music is the thing you should concentrate on because you need to escape the violence.

He was right. I had to find another way because the adventures with the AVT gang that I had joined was becoming more and more scary. I would suddenly be in fights with Glasgow Rangers fans and they were really violent with knives and hammers involved. It was pretty shocking stuff, and I needed to get away from that, and I needed to get away from this home life that was also mad. Of course, at the same time, this was all compounded by sleepless nights feeling the horror of another seizure.

So, something had to be done, and school was coming to an end. There was no point in staying on, so I applied to join a YOP scheme, which was a youth opportunity scheme, which gave young people who weren't particularly academic a chance to maybe pick up work in a trade. Initially, they started me as a car mechanic, learning how an engine works etc — something I wasn't interested in. Then, out of the blue, I was offered a job as a progress chaser with a company called Monotype for a couple of months to see how I got on, and I took to it like a duck to water.

Suddenly I felt I had my own identity. I was getting a couple of quid. I had money to go and buy albums. I could go and see Francis in the temple at the weekend. We'd go off to our favourite cinema together, which was The Cameo in Edinburgh, and see all kinds of crazy movies. Some of them were pretty mad, violent films, which for him, being a Hare Krishna monk, I always thought was a bit odd. But nonetheless, that was our ritual on a Saturday, and I would join him for lunch in the temple and have this really awful vegan food.

I started to concentrate on this opportunity that had been presented to me by Monotype, and there was a possibility that if I got focused on this there might be a job at the end of it. So, suddenly there was a chance to change my life from this sense that it was just about to explode into something really bad, into maybe something a little bit better than that.

Into The Valley

I grasped the opportunity with Monotype, who built laser-printers, mostly for the Russian market. The Dunfermline division of the company made the PC boards, and my job was to chase up the boards and get all the transformers and the lights to the people on the production line to get it done in time.

I really enjoyed it because it gave me a lot of opportunities to meet and talk to people, become part of something, another community, being with adults, which I liked very much — mostly women — and they were really great fun and very flirtatious.

At the same time it gave me a chance to sit down and read my new bible, which was music papers — the NME, the *Melody Maker* and *Sounds*. Three newspapers would come out on a Thursday, and those newspapers were so important to me, as the journalists introduced all kinds of things. From Bruce Springsteen's new album to what Bruce Springsteen's thinking about, to an interview with Graham Parker & The Rumour, to an interview with this new cool guy from New York — Mink DeVille — to where is Lou Reed headed at this point and time in his career.

It was fantastic stuff mixed, of course, always with in- depth interviews with bands like Queen, which had no interest to me whatsoever, but I would still read it all voraciously, it was a world that was really becoming part of me, in a strange way, without even realising it.

It was at that point in time that I started to go to concerts on my own, over to Edinburgh, and see bands

— The Sensational Alex Harvey Band I saw at the Usher Hall, playing support to Mott the Hoople, then Steve Harley and Cockney Rebel, Leonard Cohen, Graham Parker, Southside Johnny and many more. I liked just going on my own. Some of them I didn't like very much, some I did; but

Into The Valley

I was much happier just being alone.

Suddenly I felt I had found the exit from the violence and from the insanity, and it was music that seemed to guide me. It was just very simple. Just go to concerts, go to record stores, read music newspapers, listen to John Peel, and the most important thing I had to do next was find a new place to live, and I did that.

I managed to move into a house in Dunfermline, where I lived in the attic. They had no room in the house but they rented me the attic for not very much money, and it was pretty cool. I changed it into a mad, fairly idiosyncratic place which was covered in posters of everything from Spiderman through to Bela Lugosi, all the way through to *Born to Run* by Bruce Springsteen, and images of David Bowie, Roxy Music — The New York Dolls, and of course the mighty Lou Reed.

So I had my own space with my own record player, my own music, and I could afford to pay the rent. I had a job. I remember coming out of that place feeling really strong and independent. I was still only sixteen years old.

Into The Valley

CHAPTER NINE

My vague memories of the summer of 1976 was of a heat wave. Even up in Scotland the sun just bored down on you and there was rationing going on with water supplies. A new thing to experience. And there was something in the air. There was definitely something in the air; a sense of frustration, youth unemployment, industrial action was pretty much a daily event with big strikes breaking out everywhere.

The music that was reflecting this just didn't seem to be there. The music that was political, the music that in some way we as young people could relate to just wasn't there.

Most of the pop stars at that time were just awful. At one end you had rock bands who were so removed from their audience and sang songs about peculiar, somewhat idiotic subject matters from goblins to their own version of misogyny and sexism. Even politically there was a sense that the political class had no idea what it was like to be a young person in 1976 under this blazing sunshine with a sense of just not being attached to anything of any value.

And then it happened. The first I got a sense of something big going on was when the tabloid newspapers like *The Sun* and the *Daily Mirror*, the *Daily Mail*, the *Daily Express*, suddenly put on their front pages this new thing that was going on primarily in London called punk rock, and the Sex

Pistols, who I had already heard about via the John Peel Show.

In his own visionary way he must have smelt something was going on with these new bands and their anti-establishment, anti-authoritarian outlook on life. But nobody had really heard their music and suddenly there they were on all the front pages, the filth and the fury.

These new young people were out there mocking and laughing at the establishment and these well-held views that had gone on from generation to generation were suddenly being satirised. Of course, these stupid media outlets were looking for a shock horror element, and they provided the new bands with a chance to promote what should have been an underground movement, into the faces of the nation.

It all seemed to play into the hands of us in the outreaches, the frontiers people who were a million miles away from the heat of central London, in the sense of that's where it was going on. In sleepy Dunfermline, the Sex Pistols were announced in the daily newspapers but all but vanished immediately.

But there were a few of us that had hooked onto something that was exciting, something we could relate to. Then we started to hear the music coming through John Peel, through various sessions and hearing him talking about these bands he was going to see.

Those of us who were listening to that late-night show knew that a combination of the media furore and this new dynamic music that just punched you straight in the face was politicised — was rich in opinion, and reflected the world that was going on around it, that connected with young people immediately and a sense of its despair, disenfranchisement, and a dislocation from what was regarded as society. All of these things, all of these pieces came together immediately in the late summer of '76.

It was like life had just started. The combination of hearing music by The Clash and at the same time watching the Notting Hill riots and the sense of Joe Strummer's lyrics and Mick Jones' guitar riffs were reflecting that in some way. For me all of the things that had gone on in the past, the music I had listened to, Lou Reed, David Bowie, Roxy Music, MC5, Iggy Pop, New York Dolls, all suddenly made sense. It was like somebody had cooked the perfect pie and I just had to bite into it. But how did we get these records, we couldn't walk into a store like Rough Trade in London or any of these other more progressive record stores.

We were stuck here in the east of Scotland where these things didn't really exist until two things happened around that time. One was a guy called Bruce Findlay who started his own record stores predictably called *Bruce's* which existed for a while. But instead of turning his back on punk rock like most of the major record store chains, he did the opposite.

He was suddenly helping promote bands that were coming up to play in Edinburgh and selling tickets from his shops and allowing young people like myself and other like-minded people to hang out in his shop as a hub. There were two stores. One was in the west end of Edinburgh, the other where I hung out was in a back street called Rose Street which had a reputation as being a place where prostitutes worked and it had gay bars, so it was a slightly transgressive part of Edinburgh life.

Bruce's was on that street which made his shop even cooler. And just outside the station there was Coburn Street which to this day remains an alternative street and at the top of the road was *City Records* and they too adopted punk.

They suddenly were importing records from the States,

obscure 12 inches, from Patti Smith, MC5 and Iggy Pop. You'd go into there and they'd be playing Television's new album or *Horses* by Patti Smith, as well the new bands from Manchester, like The Buzzcocks. It's in that store that I queued for a long, long time on a Saturday morning to pick up my copy of The Damned's first album.

It was interesting that the album that I got didn't have the band on the back. There'd been a printing error and it was Eddie and the Hot Rods on the back cover, which made it a bit of a collector's item. But it was just a magic moment to have that album. To hear The Damned thrashing it out in their own camp, somewhat subversive way.

Over the back streets in the old town of Edinburgh towards Johnson Terrace there was a hippie club called Nicky-Tams that had a smell of patchouli oil and lots of people wore Wrangler bags with spaces down the sides and dressed and spoke like hippies.

But they felt some guardianship for us young punks because they allowed us to come in there with our albums on a Saturday afternoon, into early evening and play our own music and dance before the place became a full-blown hippie joint. It was actually pretty magical because the DJ would just say what do you want to play? I would bring over Television or Patti Smith or Iggy Pop and he would play it. Then of course suddenly I had my Damned album which was pretty exciting. So I'd take it from the record store over to this weird hippie club where I sat and played it.

I would sit there with Francis, who by then had left the temple and he immediately got punk. He just got it, because he's the guy who had introduced me to the New York Dolls and The Velvet Underground, so he immediately drew the connection with early Velvets and punk rock. He would sit with me or dance with me in this mental club as we played these crazy records that were suddenly coming out of London.

For the first time properly in my life I suddenly felt part of a new social group, the politics, the attitude, the clothes, the sensibility, everything about it was beginning to make sense. All the things that had almost been rammed down my throat, didn't make any sense to me. All the times of feeling different made sense because now you started to look different — this new music, the clothes, your sense of who you were. It was our identity. Looking back at the time I remember in those early days of punk I always used to wear a German national football strip with the great German football player Beckenbauer's name on the back of it. I loved that top. The white top with the black trimmings. It was only later on in life I was to discover maybe where that perverse love of the German national strip came from. Rather than wearing a Scotland strip or anything else it was because there was a huge connection with my own life with my father's family coming from Germany.

I would try to really remember why when I was a little kid I always wore the German shirt. I'm sure it's because my father used to buy it for me. I'm absolutely convinced of that. Because otherwise why would I? It must have been really difficult to find in the shops in Scotland, but I always seemed to have a German strip. To this day I still wear the national strip from that era of course, the 1970's.

My parents at this point in time were completely bewildered by this shift in my life. The summer was ending, I was about to leave school and start at a further education place called Halbeath Technical College. I lasted there for a few weeks and as previously mentioned they farmed me out to Monotype.

So suddenly, there I was, punk rock had happened, it had

made its stamp on the national psyche. I was starting to buy the albums that were coming out of London, I had a job and I was earning some money. Not a lot, but I was perfectly happy as long as I had my music papers to read; *Sounds, Melody Maker, New Musical Express*.

1976 was a massive game changer. It gave me a sense of purpose, a sense of identity; all of the things that made me feel alienated suddenly were my strength. I didn't have to try to be different. You were different. I didn't have to force myself into social groups because I didn't want to, and their rejection of me because of my epilepsy didn't really matter anymore. Suddenly being part of this movement as I thought it was, punk rock, I identified with everything, especially the music.

When I heard the *Live at the Roxy* album, I didn't like all of the music, but I still identified with everyone. Bands like Eater, who were tiny kids like I was, Arthouse, bands like Wire I loved and love to this day. I had a really amazing feel of this strange other planet which was called London and that came to be like a lighthouse from faraway. This light that was blinking and blinking and saying come on, come down, have a look, have a listen, partake, and see how you get on with it.

CHAPTER TEN

Dunfermline had a reputation for music venues and a variety of different types of music was going on pretty much every day of the week.

Mostly folk-oriented and a lot of Ceilidh, traditional Scottish stuff. But also lurking underneath that were music clubs where bands or people who were interested in playing instruments could go along and jam and do a solo thing.

It seemed an excuse to get into, or a reason to get into, a club. Because I was only 16 years old it was pretty much impossible in Scotland to get into a bar or a pub. But the music clubs were a little bit more relaxed.

So I started to hang out in these clubs, pretty much going on my own. But I cut a good figure with the clothes that I had picked up from second-hand clothes stores in Edinburgh. I had skin-tight trousers, an old evening jacket, white silk scarf and winklepicker shoes, with spiky hair and a dog collar. Bit of a cliché, of course, taking all these ideas from what was going on in London at the time and the photographs I had seen of punks. I soon got this out of my system because it felt ridiculous. But I'd go on to these music evenings and one of them was in the back bar of the Castleton Pub in the Kinema Ballroom. On a Thursday evening they opened up a part of the Kinema, which was quite a big space, as a music venue for people to get up and do their own thing.

Mostly it was pretty awful. It was long-haired, sad hippie types playing 'Stairway To Heaven' by Led Zeppelin badly, or songs which I wasn't particularly familiar with but I think they would be by bands like Jethro Tull, Wishbone Ash and the likes. This was music that meant absolutely nothing to me, and the people playing the music, in my mind, were pretty much idiots. But it was a place to go to and it was there that I first met this strange, tall, gangly, skinny guy who had these narrow, burning black eyes. He had great hair, I remember that, and a big smile. So this big, gangly, tall, skinny-looking thing came up and spoke to me. He had a cigarette sticking out of his mouth. He looked a little bit like Sid Vicious, a maybe slightly more handsome version with equally rough skin, I remember.

I had been up on the floor dancing to 'Marquee Moon' by Television on my own and he'd been watching from the side. He had a guitar with him and he was going to get up and play a few songs. He said to me, will I hang around and have a chat with him.

He played a song by Nils Lofgren and a song by Be Bop Deluxe He seemed quite accomplished. He was obviously a really good guitar player and he had a very sweet, quite melodic voice.

I spoke to him afterwards and we got on. He told me a little bit about Nils Lofgren, the kind of person he was, and told me that Be Bop Deluxe were in fact coming to play in Dunfermline in a few nights' time supported by a band he thought that I might like called Doctors of Madness fronted by someone called Kid Strange. So we agreed to hang out at that gig together.

I went off into the night thinking I've met a friend, somebody who was really interesting, and a good guitar player. He had slightly different tastes in music but was very excited by the stuff that was coming out of the punk rock scene. So a few days later I went along and managed to see Be Bop Deluxe, supported by the Doctors of Madness.

Ironically, Be Bop Deluxe were fronted by Bill Nelson, who would go on to produce one of the finest Skids records, *Days In Europa*, and become a personal friend. I would make a poetry record called *The Ballad Of Etiquette* for his own label Cocteau Records, and Bill Nelson became an enormous influence on my life as did the guy who was fronting the Doctors of Madness, someone called Kid Strange, better known as Richard Strange.

Richard and I went on to become really big, big friends and still are to this day. I performed at his cabaret surrealist dada club in London called Cabaret Futura every week. In fact, I went on tour with him around the UK and he's actually appeared in one of my films, *The Somnambulists*.

So we retained our friendship and I always had a really fantastic regard for Richard, especially after the set by the Doctors of Madness that particular evening. I thought they were fantastic, really exciting. Be Bop Deluxe were a very elegant rock band with a twist. Nelson had something about him that was a bit different from all the sad rock reptiles that were squeezing the juice out of the fans. He seemed a bit fresher and a bit more exciting than that.

I looked around to find Adamson but I didn't see him that evening, although he told me later on he was definitely there with his friend Bill Simpson. Stuart and Bill had been in a band called Tattoo that toured around the American air bases in Scotland, playing cover versions of everything from Status Quo songs to the things that they really liked, like Nils Lofgren and Be Bop Deluxe.

But I think punk rock had come along at the same time as it had done for me and created the space that they'd always been looking for, something where they could have their own identity and their own sense of their own music rather than doing cover versions.

But it was a minor moment where we bumped into each other in one of these music nights. I remember the person that organised the one where we had met was a guy called Pano who would go on to become the Skids' first manager and organise a lot of our first dates all over Scotland, north of England and London before, for some reason, we moved away from him which we should never have done because he was a fantastic guy.

A few nights later after this meeting with Adamson... Obviously there was no things like social media or mobile phones, so one could only ever speak by landline. But he had given me his number. He lived in a place called Crossgates with his mother and father and sister. I was still living in the attic of the house in Dunfermline, which was so cold. But I continued to cover it in posters and made it my own space and I loved it in its own unique way. It was the first space that was mine.

I gave Adamson a call and said I'm going to go over to Edinburgh at the weekend to a place called Clouds in the Tollcross area of Edinburgh. I'd been there a few times and on a Saturday night they let punks in and they played some new punk music. No one was particularly aggressive towards you. It felt quite safe. I asked him if he wanted to come and he agreed. We took the train over to Edinburgh and spent the whole day there.

We went to the record stores, *Bruce's* and *City Records* and listened to all this new music that was coming out of London and New York. Stuart was a big fan of reggae so we started to listen to some of that. We talked to the other people in the shops that were hanging around there and then went along to Nicky-Tams, the hippie joint where, again, we were allowed to play our own music, met up with my brother Francis, who was preparing to go to London — Stuart and Francis really got on, which endeared me to Stuart even more, and then we went off later on in the night to Clouds.

Upstairs in Clouds was a Northern Soul club where it seemed to be pretty much men only, just guys dancing to the music that they loved. We sat there for an hour or more watching these guys doing this incredible dancing which left quite a mark on me.

The idea that they could express themselves with such freedom and liberation because they loved music. None of them seemed to drink alcohol, so I have no idea how the club made any money, but they were pretty happy up there.

Downstairs was a normal club night, but the DJ was a guy called Curtis who would go on to become a friend and flatmate of mine. He was really interested in mixing it up, so right in the middle of some horrible, cheesy 1970s disco crap, he would suddenly slip in a bit of Iggy Pop, bit of David Bowie, bit of Lou Reed and some of the new stuff, of course, that was coming thick and fast at us. It made Clouds a real destination of choice.

We had a great night in there, met some like-minded people who came with us to the train station, Waverley, where we waited for the first train back to Dunfermline, sat there from about one, till six in the morning, just talking to people. Talking to some new girls we had met who were into punk — were really cool and looked amazing and were very brave because it was so dangerous still to wander around the streets looking like we did. But we had such a great time just hanging around the station.

I think on this particular evening, where I'd spent the whole day with Adamson, was the moment where we really bonded. He said to me that he and Bill were going to redevelop their band into something a bit more fiery and real and they wanted to find a singer.

I said, "well, why don't you sing? You've got such a great voice." He said "it's too soft and that it needs to be a bit tougher than that" and he said "we want a frontman. Why don't you give it a go?" "I can't really sing and I don't know if I've got the charisma to be a frontman," I told him.

He convinced me to have a go and arranged an audition in Cowdenbeath Working Men's Club, This was a traditional place for ex-coal miners to have a beer, smoke their cigarettes and just stare into the wilderness. It was quite a sad place and they were in for bit of a shock this particular afternoon. When I turned up there were a couple of other guys waiting to audition.

One of them was Stuart's friend, a guy called Conn who had this Bryan Ferry look about him. I turned up with my regulation winklepickers, skin tight trousers and evening jacket on. I had a confidence that maybe a 16-year-old shouldn't have had at that point in time.

I had brought along a copy of 'Raw Power' by Iggy Pop and asked if I could do that at the audition. We quickly learned it and off we went. We played the song and it was pretty bad. I mean, it was about as bad as it could be, trying to impersonate the great Iggy Pop. But I performed it rather than sang it, and I think that's what stuck with them. Bill Simpson reminds me often that he said that I couldn't sing and it certainly looked like I couldn't dance, but I could perform and had a presence. So that was it, really. I thought they would have gone with their friend Conn, a very handsome guy with his slick Bryan Ferry look. But it was wrong for punk. Maybe later on when all that New Romantic crap happened, but not then. They needed something a little bit more aggressive and edgy and demented.

To describe myself at that moment in time, picture this. It was a brutal winter after this incredibly violently hot summer and I was standing there with no shirt on and with an evening jacket with winklepicker shoes, no socks and short trousers that were tight as tight could be, with grey skin and eyes popping out of my head. I looked like I'd fallen off the back of a truck from the back streets of New York without ever having to take the drugs that went along with that particular lifestyle.

It was just how I looked because of a variety of different things. I was obviously working very hard to maintain my job because I wanted that money to buy records, but also, I was still incredibly sick most of the time and really hadn't had a proper night's sleep for years and years. So, that haunted look played into the whole punk thing and it just seemed to work.

The most important fact really was that I was genuinely 16-years-old, loved the whole attitude, loved the atmosphere, loved the music, the energy, the politics and the stage, having an opportunity to have a voice, to have something to say. So they eventually asked me, if I wanted to be the singer in the band. My immediate response was, yes, I do. I really want to be the singer in this band and that was it. Stuart said, "well, let's write some songs."

Into The Valley

CHAPTER ELEVEN

Stuart and I started to go to gigs together, constantly. Any band that was coming to play in the local area, or Edinburgh, or as far afield as Falkirk and even Glasgow, we would try and get to see them.

New bands were starting all over the place and we kept an eye on some of the bands coming out of Edinburgh. Matt Vinyl and the Decorators (terrible name); The Valves, a kind of R&B band, very accomplished, and from Falkirk The Jolt, but really, in the area where we came from, we were the only punk band — The Skids.

There was nothing else really going on in the local Fife area; we were it. So, at the weekend we would disappear off to Edinburgh and see the first ever Damned gig there, which was extraordinary in a comic book-madness, kind of way, but both Stuart and I were very confused with it. We thought punk had more value than the comedy and Captain Sensible and Dave Vanian had taken it into some almost graphic novel like performance — we loved it but were still pretty uncomfortable with it.

The outstanding gig we went to during that period was the White Riot Tour which featured The Clash, The Jam, The Slits and Subway Sect. I absolutely loved Subway Sect; I thought that Vic Godard was an incredible front man and I loved their shoe-gazing self-indulgence. The Jam were pretty electric; they just performed their songs, but the punk audience in Edinburgh Playhouse had a very negative view of them. The Slits were a mess, they've now gone on to be depicted in history as one of the coolest bands of all time, but actually live, they were just a crazy noisy mess.

Viv Albertine who I worked with later on, was pretty cool, but we thought their songs were rubbish.

The Clash were majestic; they were terrifyingly brilliant and put the rest of us in our place. Stuart and I left that gig knowing that we had to up our game and really start to try and define who we were. We had been making our own clothes up to then; making our own shirts, customising our own trousers, giving ourselves a very particular look, but we suddenly realised it was all very sub-Clash.

Our new songs we had been rehearsing regularly. We worked in a garage complex just on the outskirts of Dunfermline, in a place called Wellwood and we had our own little space which the owner of the local big house allowed us to use. In that space I was constantly getting electric shocks off the microphone and it was always feeding back and giving us all searing headaches because it was so loud.

We went through all of the songs that Stuart wrote; Stuart wrote everything at that point. He wrote the music, the words, he did the structure, he wrote the drum parts, the bass parts, and obviously the vocal parts at the beginning. He was undoubtedly the band leader. So, we did his songs; things like 'Sick Club'; 'Nationwide'; 'Victims of the Weekend'. They were soon joined by songs like 'Reasons' and 'Test Tube Babies'.

All of Stuart's work in the early stages of The Skids have a social conscience; he was very aware of the world around him and how he saw the unfairness of that world. He had a social realist approach to song-writing and at the heart of all of his songs was a political sensibility. He was definitely like the rest of us, a Labour-voting left-winger; virtually everybody we knew in Scotland was left wing in those years and he used the songs as a platform to get his views across.

On average then, the life of the band would be hanging around the rehearsal space; setting up, going through new songs. Sometimes, Stuart got very impatient with the other guys because they weren't doing what he was asking them to do, but he was always very good with me. I never pretended to be a good singer and knew I was bringing an attitude to the role, but my sense of timing and melody were very weak. So he was very kind and generous with me throughout the Skids lifespan. I think at this point in time, we were pretty close. We had forged a very strong friendship based on music. I was a voracious reader and loved talking to him about the new ideas and stories I had recently read.

I explained to him about my health condition and how sometimes I just needed to disappear for a while and he understood that and was always very sympathetic and careful with me. We shared books; he was into a different type of literature from me. I was probably more pretentious and was interested in reading Aldous Huxley, probably because of David Bowie's influence; John-Paul Sartre; Albert Camus... All these books which I had heard about from the people that I liked, Lou Reed, Bowie, or early Roxy Music. They were talking about books that meant something to them and had influenced them. I felt I also had to read them because that lay at the source of the mystery of performance. This is the stuff I needed to read... So we shared these things; we talked about this stuff after rehearsals which would go on for a long time, sometimes long into the night even in a brutally cold Scottish winter.

Into The Valley

We would wander down to the pubs in the centre of Dunfermline, but most of the time, I would be asked to leave because I was still 16. They knew it and they didn't want me in there. Occasionally, we would manage to sneak in. We were never heavy drinkers or drug-taking types. We just spent our time talking about books, music and of course, because of the band, we had started to garner this little following in Dunfermline with people of the same age, who started to hang out with us.

So, we had our own little gang around us which made life a lot easier because it was still potentially dangerous looking like the way we did and carrying our guitars and no-one had seen anything like it in this quiet area before.

Suddenly, there we were, in people's faces and we were growing in popularity. I think some people probably didn't like that idea or this new movement, which they clearly didn't understand. Its tentacles were spreading out into the local schools and lots of the young kids were coming to our rehearsal space and listening to what we were doing. Without even realising it, we had become a minor cult in the area with our own following. The rehearsal space was always pretty full.

By then we had Pano looking after us. He was a biker and he was pretty much involved with the local central Scotland biker movement which I believe was quite big. He had that aura and mystery that those guys have... That they might be quite dangerous, quite tough and he certainly spun a story or two about some of his experiences at various festivals, the dynamic betweendifferent biker gangs and the violence that ensued because of that. These are the kind of stories that as a young guy, you just loved being near as it added to the excitement.

Pano came on board as our manager and started to

organise a few gigs which was a terrifying thought. That actually after all these rehearsals we were about to start playing live, regularly. The process of song-writing and the interior dynamic of the band; all that friendship and hanging around and the camaraderie which had grown and grown and grown as we went off to see other groups was now heading in a scary direction.

The time had come for us to present ourselves to an audience for the first time ever, as a live band — a really terrifying thought. One of the various problems I was having at that time, was remembering all of Stuart's words. There were so many of them; he wrote really memorable choruses for sure, but the words in the verses were long and quite detailed and I just really couldn't remember any of them off by heart. That was my first real sense of terror; how the hell am I going to perform these words? It was suggested that I would have to Sellotape all the lyric sheets onto the various mic stands and monitors, etc, so I could read them as I sang them.

It is interesting to me now that, that's what worried me at the time, not the fact that I was going to be singing in front of a live audience. I was going to be performing in a way that I had never done before and been seen as the focal point of a band. I just didn't want to mess up, and I think that is down to my respect for the other guys at the time — Stuart Adamson, Bill Simpson and Thomas Kellichan. I didn't want to let them down because I still saw myself as a bit of a fraud. These guys

Into The Valley

all had a talent... Tom could actually play the drums and keep time; Bill was a very accomplished bass player and Stuart was a magical guitar player, so who the hell was I in amongst all of this? The only way I could, in some way, alleviate the sense of worthlessness, was to make sure that when I was in front of a microphone, even in rehearsals, it was a performance.

I once read an interview with Iggy Pop where he said that if he just came in and went through the motions, the band rehearsals were absolutely terrible. But if he performed like he was on stage then the band would respond and the rehearsals would take off. That's what it was like in our small garage space. Funny to think back, but we really were a garage band. I wonder if The Clash ever actually rehearsed in a real garage? I don't think so.

CHAPTER TWELVE

The first ever Skids' gig in 1977, was at the Bellville Hotel in the centre of Dunfermline. On the second floor was a music club, which normally put on folk acts and softer music. It was the place where they had wedding receptions and birthday parties. Pano had started to become the promoter for this venue so it made sense that it would become our first gig. The hotel from the outside looks quite formidable. It still stands there today. It's now called Johnson's. It has a really quite cool feel about it, lots of glass, steep and tall.

For us, tiny little guys from Nowheresville, suddenly playing our first ever gig, became somewhat terrifying because we had rehearsed and rehearsed and rehearsed, but suddenly, there we were getting ready to actually play to a real audience, a paying audience. The hotel space was very intimidating because residents were milling around, and there we were these odd-looking feral punks carrying our equipment up the stairs for their debut gig.

We had prepared quite intensively for the gig, rehearsing as much as we possibly could within the parameters of our various jobs. Rehearsing in the evening after we finished, rehearsing at the weekends, for hours and hours. We felt we were pretty tight, although from my own point of view, having never sang live before in front of an audience, it was completely unknown territory.

Stuart and Bill of course, had played many times with Tattoo, but it was something that I had never imagined was going to happen, yet the day had come. I'm not sure if I was nervous because I don't think I've ever been nervous before a show, that never really affected me in that way. But I was concerned that I didn't let the other guys down. I was concerned that I couldn't remember the lyrics of Stuart's songs and that I would make a mess of the whole thing. I didn't ever want to come across as somebody who is overly professional or slick. But at the same time, I didn't want to make myself look like an idiot and most importantly I didn't want to let Stuart and Bill down.

We managed to get up the stairs and start to prepare for a sound check, but we weren't allowed to do that because the residents didn't want to hear this incredible noise spiralling down the stairs where they were sitting, having afternoon tea or a drink in the bar. But we forged on and did our sound check anyway and there was definitely a tension in the air. Everybody felt that this was a big moment because if it didn't go well, then maybe it would be the end of the band.

We had only really settled on a name a few months before. There was various ideas about what the name should be and they were all ridiculous, comic-book and idiotic. But we liked the name Skids because it had a social-realist feel about it, being on the skids. And really, the world around us felt like that. So we, as a band with that name, were a reflection of the social disorder of the local community and the wider industrial areas of Central Scotland.

Word of mouth was roaring around the town and beyond, and there was a good uptake on ticket sales, so we knew it was going to be a busy night. It was a music club night anyway, so there were regulars who came there. We talked about how we were going to present the songs. Stuart at that point in time since he was the writer, was perfectly happy to do introductions, something that I'd never even considered; that I was going to have to introduce these songs, maybe talk about them, have a relationship with the audience. I think I was more concerned about how I looked and what was going to be the image of the band on stage.

Tom Kellichan had renamed himself as Tom Bomb, which was a bit daft. We all changed our names. Stuart was Stevie Cologne, Bill was Alex Plode, which was pretty good, and I had the idiotic name of Joey Jolson, which I have no idea where that came from. We abandoned those names and took ourselves as seriously as we could, although Tom had Tom Bomb emblazoned on his cut down denim jacket. I stuck with my tight trousers, winkle pickers and black evening jacket. I had dyed my hair black at the time with a white stripe down the side, which was my pride and joy. It made me stand out from the crowd and feel different and look visually different from the people who were following the band or many of the punks that we had met and hang out with in Edinburgh and Glasgow.

The rest of the band didn't think too hard about how

they looked, they just wanted to get on with it. Stuart had this customized Clash-esque shirt on. Bill, I think had white overalls on, which were very similar to one of the Droogs from *Clockwork Orange*. We sat nervously backstage hearing the din of the people in the crowd screaming and shouting at one another. I remember peering around the curtains to where the audience had assembled, and some of them I recognised as people who had been hanging out with the band at the rehearsal space. There were people I had met at various bars and events in Edinburgh and some old school chums who had come along to support this new, crazy endeavour.

But there was also a bunch of new people there that I had never seen before and they had a very different look from the rest of us. They had long hair, moustaches, and I wondered if they were some of Pano's biker friends. They had that vibe about them. So there was two very different tribes in the room which offered up potential problems we had not foreseen. I reported this information to the rest of the band and it only seemed to make them even more nervous.

Looking at Stuart, Bill and Tom on that evening, made me realise how young we were because they looked so incredibly vulnerable and scared. But nonetheless, we had to get on with it. So we wandered onto the stage. Stuart introduced who we were, I introduced the first song, and off we went. Playing 100 miles an hour, a song called 'Nationwide', which Stuart had written about local gangs and how people of our generation were just so bored; the only way that they found comfort and leisure was through indiscriminate violence towards one another. It was a song that reflected the idiocy of actions that were very normal in our environment.

But the words were lost in the madness that ensued in front of me as we kicked off. I had all my lyrics stuck on the microphone stand with Sellotape, but people had already stolen them or knocked them off or ripped them in half. I was suddenly put in the position where I just had to remember the words or improvise which became yet another piece of tension that I just didn't need on this particular evening, the band's debut gig.

From the very first song the crowd was jumping up and down; staring and pointing and throwing shadow punches at us, and it definitely felt like it was going to end up as a violent melee. But somehow, it was just young people caught up in the angst and anger and rage of the songs. Nonetheless, I did notice that those standing at the side of the stage with the greasy long hair and moustaches, denim gear on and big biker boots, were not enjoying us at all. They really didn't like us. They seemed to be Pano's friends because he was hanging out with them but it still felt like if there was going to be any danger that evening, it was going to come from them.

The set progressed and we calmed down when Stuart introduced a song called '*Scared to Dance*', which would go on to become the title of our first album. It was a much more rock-oriented song, although the lyrics were pretty tough. It's about a person shadowing a young woman towards a potential attack, if not a rape. The title had been taken from an article written by Tony Parsons about young people in Poland during the communist regime in 1976, and how they were scared to dance. Stuart had readapted the idea and applied it to the violence of the area that we came from and how it was really dangerous to be young, especially if you were a woman.

The biker gang seemed to appreciate this song more than the others because it had a guitar solo and it had a different feel to the 100 mile an hour thrash songs we were doing. It certainly calmed them down a bit but the potential for violence was there. The potential for the whole thing to go terribly wrong, was there. But somehow we managed to get through it. As we approached the last song of the set, we definitely got the feeling that this was the beginning of something, given that we had survived our first gig. It wasn't an amazing success; it wasn't something we could have anticipated in any way. In many ways, it just was what it was: Us confronting the audience and the audience confronting us. But it went off without any terrible violence.

We came off the stage feeling confident that, yes, this idea, this project, this creative process we had entered, maybe had some mileage in it. It wasn't going to begin and end on one evening. It was going to go further than that. For me personally, it was a magnificent event for different reasons. Primarily because the camaraderie of the band was something that I had always looked for in different areas of my life from being so isolated because of my health condition and I'd never really found it. I hadn't really found it in the world of football or hooliganism or gang life. I felt like I had stuck myself onto that world to try and fit in, to try and be like other people, and that was a mistake.

Now, I wasn't trying to fit in or be like anybody else. I was just being myself and I was completely appreciated for that. People spoke to us after the gig and the general consensus was that we were pretty good and I had delivered the goods as a front man and I had a presence. As a group we looked like we wanted to take this somewhere further. We wanted to advance, get better and improve. Most importantly, it looked like we were friends. We were a different type of gang. We were a music gang. We were people who wanted to use this platform in a creative way. We had found our voice.

CHAPTER THIRTEEN

The reaction to the first-ever Skids gig in the Bellville Hotel in Dunfermline was pretty much instantaneous. The word spread around the local area very, very quickly that there was a new band in town. Some people of course absolutely hated us — Thought we were the most repulsive, unmusical thing they've ever heard in their life, but they were normally old. Young people just embraced it.

Punk was, by this time, spreading into the younger generation like a firestorm. They were beginning to see bands, hear bands, be able to buy singles and albums by bands that in many ways reflected the world as they saw it. And the Skids were one of those bands.

It suddenly became the case that we couldn't play enough gigs. We wanted to play more and more and more. It was difficult because we were still trying to hold down jobs so we could pay for all of this but the thirst was there and the demand was there. But the venues weren't. Pano, tried his best to get us into as many different towns in Scotland as possible to play, but it became problematic for a variety of reasons. Many of the promoters didn't want to book us because we were associated with this new movement, Punk. And we weren't, in their mind, musical enough to play in their traditional flavoured venues, which didn't really accept this new type of music.

The other thing that was at play was how political we were. The songs were about what was going on in the world. The disenfranchisement from the establishment. The sense of worthlessness in their eyes.

We did gigs in Edinburgh as part of the Anti-Nazi League. One of the gigs that happened soon after the Bellville was a Chilean refugee benefit concert in Dunfermline, down the glen, which was organised by the local Communist Party. This ended in tears of course because Stuart stood up after playing two or three of our songs which were going down pretty well in this outdoor gig, and told the audience that if this was a communist country, you wouldn't be allowed to listen to a band like the Skids.

The plug was literally pulled immediately by the organisers and all hell let loose. Punches and kicks were being thrown in every direction and the police eventually arrived and arrested Stuart, Pano and myself. We were not charged with anything but we were given a stern warning to stay out of their sights.

It was really a sign for us, every day seemed to bring another page-turning event of some kind. Things we hadn't experienced before and of course, we were beginning to meet other bands who were like minded.

There was a young band from Edinburgh called the Scars who we were very fond of. Their guitar player and Stuart got on very well and their singer had a real personality and charisma about him and their songs were a little bit more left field than ours, a bit artier.

By this time, we were starting to support the big bands. So, in our favourite club in Edinburgh, Clouds, we suddenly were supporting the Buzzcocks. The mighty Buzzcocks. We were so excited about playing with them but we were treated appallingly by Pete Shelley and Steve Diggle. They were really just a couple of arseholes who were really drunk and looked down their nose at us, weren't interested and didn't give us a soundcheck. We were so disappointed because we thought the punk movement as we saw it, was all about camaraderie and friendship and generosity. But they just didn't give a shit. We were a bit naive.

The Buzzcocks were a pop band really. I liked their songs but their attitude to it was just about the kick. About the instantaneous kick. They wanted to be almost like old-fashioned pop stars, which was hugely disappointing.

We supported The Clash at the Kinema Ballroom in Dunfermline and they actually made us go on stage before the doors opened. So, when the hundreds of young people ran in, we were already into our set. But it didn't stop people going crazy and jumping about and going mad as we played. I looked to the side of the stage where Mick Jones and Joe Strummer were watching us. We managed to talk to them for a while afterwards. They were very supportive. Both of them. Joe Strummer remained a friend as did Mick. Sadly, Joe is no longer with us. I really miss him.

Richard Hell and the Voidoids were the main support act that evening. He was a 24-carat tosser and brought an American viciousness to the table which was very camp, hysterical and pretty un-frightening to us. We saw through it straight away. That it was all a theatrical thing that was going on and we were pretty unimpressed. But it was an amazing situation where suddenly we were now the band of choice in Scotland. Supporting the bands either from the States or from the big cities in England.

We were the band that was chosen to support them. Certainly in the East and sometimes in the West of Scotland.

As you'll understand we thought that maybe we should start considering making a record. We were taking part in a competition for Stiff Records, they wanted to find new acts and were trawling up and down the country on a tour. The local bands got a chance to come and do a couple of gigs supporting some of the bigger acts. But they weren't particularly interested in the Skids, so we decided to go on with our own thing.

We went into a studio in Edinburgh called REL and we could really ill afford to be there. It was a brand-new experience being in a proper, professional studio but at the same time, we didn't really have time to think about it. We just had to get in. Set our gear up. Do some very basic soundcheck and then just get on with playing as if it was a live performance which actually played into our hands. We were doing Stuart's locally classic 'Test Tube Babies' which was a fun, edgy pop song with a serious social message.

We also recorded a new classy song he'd been working on which was about automation in industry and how the old-fashioned, traditional male role was becoming obsolete. The song was called 'Charles' and it felt really sophisticated. It wasn't like the 100-mile-an-hour songs that were being done by everybody else. It had a very peculiar, idiosyncratic sound that was a new thing that Stuart was developing with his guitar playing, which was with an open string. Some people thought it sounded like bagpipes. But essentially that was a technique that he'd developed and 'Charles' was one of the first songs that came out of that — maybe 'Charles' and a song called 'Of One Skin'. We got into the studio and recorded these songs really quickly.

The experience was, in many ways, not something that we could revel in because we just didn't have time to. We just had to treat it like any other event and hope that the person who was engineering the session caught what the band were all about. It was an amazing sequence of events:

writing, rehearsing, recording and then within a month this record appears that we made on that particular day with its own sleeve on our own label, No Bad Records, which is the label we still use to this day. I was very excited.

I think the name No Bad came from Pano. No bad in the east of Scotland means it's not great, but it's not terrible. It's just cool. It fitted what we were all about and had an element of humility and at the same time, it had its own particular style.

That's what we had been developing, you can feel it in the music, hear it in the sound and suddenly we were moving further afield. We were going down to places like Manchester and hanging out for the weekend. We supported the Rezillos down there in a club called Rafters. We hung out at the Ranch Club that evening. Played with Slaughter and the Dogs. We met a band called Warsaw who were, of course, to become Joy Division. That was the first time I met Ian Curtis who became a friend of sorts.

The tentacles of the band were pushing out but the most exciting thing that had happened was that we had our own record on our own label. That's really where things changed overnight for us because all of the momentum from playing live, being brave, forceful and aggressive when we were performing and not being afraid to support these big bands, really all came together in this first record.

Suddenly at 11 o'clock at night there was John Peel playing his favourite new record which was 'Charles' by the Skids. A band from Dunfermline in Fife in Scotland and he really loved that record. He played it and played it.

It was so exciting to be a young guy suddenly listening to this music that you had made being played by this legendary DJ. Somebody who had introduced you to so many different types of music. Who had been such an influence in your life and there he was playing your music saying it was good and that he really loved this band and wanted to know more about them. That was the moment, I think, that the band, our future, everything we were about, changed forever.

CHAPTER FOURTEEN

So what was my relationship like with Stuart Adamson as the Skids began to develop? From being a bunch of kids rehearsing in a garage in a back street in Dunfermline, to suddenly being a band that was garnering attention from wherever we played, be it in the surrounding areas from where we were from in central Scotland or further north, down south as far as Manchester and of course we were now travelling as far afield as London as well.

The success of the support of John Peel had made the Skids a band that people were suddenly aware of; we weren't just from a rural backwater in Scotland, we were the guys that wrote the song 'Charles', or at least Stuart Adamson was the guy that wrote 'Charles' and we were the guys that played on it.

It really got a lot of attention; it was very well received. People commented on its uniqueness and there was a sense of expectation about this new band because punk had become very derivative. A lot of the bands that were emerging at the same time as us were direct copies of the Clash or the Ramones or even the Sex Pistols.

There was nothing particularly unique about them, they didn't have their own style, they didn't have their own stamp, their own voice; they were just copycat bands. But because of this recording, which was played pretty much every night by John Peel, the Skids suddenly had a very clear identity, and that identity was undoubtedly given to us through the guitar playing and song writing, at this stage at least, by Stuart Adamson.

My friendship with him had grown and grown. We started to share a room together when we went to various other places, be it Manchester or London, and we were pretty much in each other's company 24/7. We were hanging out together all the time, before gigs, after gigs, in the hotels. During the day we'd go to the cinema together, see movies and catch up on different films, talk about books, share different ideas.

Stuart was heavily politicised. He loved Dunfermline Athletic; I think it irritated him that I wasn't a Dunfermline Athletic fan. I was a Celtic fan which he never really understood but it was a cultural thing, which is interesting in itself because Scotland was famously divided along sectarian lines during the 1970s. The east of Scotland didn't have it so bad but it still existed, and the Skids were a really good example of how that just didn't work for us.

We weren't interested in that because Tom, Bill and Stuart were all Protestants and of course I was a Catholic. We never discussed it once. It was not something we talked about even though there were atrocities going on from the Loyalist and Republican forces in Northern Ireland, which were being imported into the mainland: Certainly more in the south of England, in London especially and of course Birmingham and Guildford.

It was something we were very aware of but it never became, at any point in time, something that was a contrary feeling or emotion within the band. We had a very derisory view of any form of sectarianism and bigotry, we hated it.

But he did love his local football team, Dunfermline

Athletic, and went to see them as much as possible. I did go along with him and Bill occasionally to watch them. They weren't very good, but I admired the fact that they supported and had a passion for their local team. When we went away we shared rooms and even discussed family elements. Stuart asked me a lot about my family, he was very friendly with my older brother John who he liked immensely. John was a great football player and also a very, very funny guy.

Stuart loved being in his company because he told fantastically funny stories and characterised a lot of the local people in a really wonderful way, which often had Stuart rolling about the floor laughing. He was also aware of my very strong relationship with Francis and he was one of the few people I met in my life who understood that Francis was a special person and was not some crazy guy. He was somebody who had taken a very difficult route that most people would never understand, into a completely alternative lifestyle. But he admired that.

So we became very close in that sense; we would talk about our families. Stuart alluded to something dark in his family life and without ever getting to the absolute rub of it; it definitely had something to do with his relationship with his father.

It was around this time where we were more intimate in our friendship that he started to involve me in the writing. He read some of the poetry I'd been writing and looked at some of my notebooks and started to try and put these crazy, mad words to music. The first, being the song I actually wrote about him, which was 'Of One Skin'.

The words that he shared with me and the stories he told me became some of the lyrics I used in that first song. 'Of One Skin' is an example of a song from those experiences that we still play to this date. If you were to really analyse the lyrics and apply them to Stuart's life, then you would see that those lyrics were in many ways a biographical sketch of some of the stuff that Stuart told me that was going on or had gone on in his life.

We were young guys in a world that seemed to be excited by our presence, but we never had outrageous egos or were arrogant about what we were doing. We kept a steady head, I think, throughout the whole period. We weren't big drinkers, we didn't drink spirits, and we'd occasionally have the odd beer. I think Stuart occasionally liked a little puff of some dope, but it's not something I ever got involved with.

I told him in detail about some of the problems I was having with my health; about not being able to sleep at night, having these weird seizures and fainting fits. He was very aware that I had things going wrong and the fact that I looked sick all of the time. He always thought it was funny because it added to the image of the band in many ways, to have a singer who looked like a junkie who had never done a drug in his life was deeply ironic in his view.

The more time we spent together hanging out in the cinema, bookshops or occasionally going to a bar, the more we talked about these odd, elaborate lyrics. I thought it was crazy that he would be interested in using my words, because he was such a great lyric writer and his stuff is a social commentary.

But he really pushed and pushed me to try stuff. I was staying with a guy called Johnny Waller, on the outskirts of Dunfermline where I rented a room. Stuart would come round there with his guitar and start trying to put my crazy lyrics to a tune and they became these epic, abstract songs that appeared in our live set: 'Scale', 'Zit', and 'Six Times' or even a song which was more about my own paranoia about being in the band, called 'Integral Plot'. I wrote that when I felt the other guys were actually conspiring to get rid of me because I wasn't really a very good singer. I had no natural musical ability, and maybe I was a liability because I was still a pretty crazy person at the time. I looked so ill that maybe they didn't think I was going to be around for much longer.

Sometimes I think my onstage presence made the other guys concerned that I was borderline insane. I often thought they would try and get rid of me, and replace me with someone else, so 'Integral Plot' became a reflection of that adolescent paranoia. We still stuck pretty closely together and even though the attention was growing and growing, I think our love of music and love of other bands kept us away from being self- indulgent.

We went to see bands as many times as we could, sometimes two or three times a week, and felt we could even learn from watching even some of the bad groups. There was this growing feeling that the Skids were definitely going somewhere and there was lots of record company interest coming from London. Our concern about where this might go in the future was actually becoming something palpable, something like… We could really do something, we could really say something, and we could really become a band doing something that was important.

So, all of these things were manifesting themselves at the same time; all the electricity of friendship and trying new things, and paranoia and sharing secrets with one another. It was really what was at the heart of an amazing friendship. That connection stayed with us, up until really the point in time when I introduced Stuart to a girl who worked with me at the factory I worked in at Monotype. Her name was Sandra, and from the first moment he met her, he fell in love with her. She became his girlfriend very quickly, and there was no doubt in his mind that she was going to become his wife and the mother of their children.

In a strange way, the incredible bond we had created changed again at that moment. I think Stuart was always looking for the friendship of a relationship that was more emotional… That had more of that intimacy, towards having a stable home and a family, and all of the things he dreamed of having. These of course were things that I'd never considered; I didn't really expect to be alive for much longer. Just take each day and run with it, was my feeling.

CHAPTER FIFTEEN

After the various gigs we had done in London, and the buzz about the band around the rest of the country, there was a lot of interest from different record companies. The one that really seemed the most prominent and the coolest to us was Virgin Records. They were the most enthusiastic; they had the best feel for the band; they understood the dynamic at the heart of it. They wanted us to push on and take that energy and music into the studio, and try and create a studio sound that was uniquely the Skids, but at the same time become something that was commercial and could invite another audience — an even younger audience, to become part of the whole Skids story.

The central person at the heart of this, beyond Richard Branson, was a guy called Simon Draper. Simon would be the person who would really be advisory counsel through the A&R Department to the band, through all of our periods with Virgin. The Skids made their second record with Virgin Records after our own label, No-Bad, and we made all of our records afterwards with Virgin. Up until now, of course, where we've gone back full circle to using our own label, No- Bad, for our 2018 album *Burning Cities*.

Simon was a very nice guy. I think we were slightly intimidated by the people we met in Virgin. They all seemed very laid-back, a little bit hippie-ish. This was the label, after all, of Mike Oldfield and Steve Hillage, and also a lot of great reggae acts. But Simon seemed completely switched on to what we were trying to do and of course, Virgin had taken the Sex Pistols when nobody else would touch them, and released Never Mind the Bollocks, to great success. They'd also signed other bands like Penetration from Newcastle, who were big friends of ours, and XTC.

So rather than just jumping on the bandwagon and signing anybody, the Virgin team led by Simon seemed to be looking for bands who, at their heart, had melodies and music, and had the potential to have a future that they could evolve beyond the fury and the volley and thunder of punk rock.

Simon Draper dealt with us immediately, and I think we had a big connection with him. He was a thoroughly decent man. He was from a different world to us. He was obviously from quite a privileged background. He was very comfortable with life, incredibly handsome as well, so he had the world at his feet. He had the most beautiful woman I think I've ever seen, Dominique Bertrand, working with him, who was French. I fell in love with her the first day I saw her. I had no chance. She went on to marry Roger Taylor from Queen.

So it was quite an overwhelming experience going into his office to have our first ever meeting with Virgin Records, down a little mews just off Portobello Road in West London, called Vernon Yard. We arrived on the first train of the day from Edinburgh, which took about seven hours in those days.

We remained pretty sane and had great fun on the way down. Stuart definitely felt Virgin was the best thing for us. We were joined by Pano and the man who had released and funded No-Bad Records, Sandy Muir, who owned the local music store, and seemed to be coming part of our management set-up as he had a little bit more business experience.

Unfortunately Pano was being increasingly pushed into the background. Pano and Clive Ford, who was our long-serving roadie had been with us from day one and were part of the family. They knew as much about the band and the individuals' various problems, idiosyncrasies and delicacies as anybody else on this planet. But somehow or other, we were being advised, not particularly discreetly, that it was time to move on. Because this Virgin deal, if it was to be signed, was a moment to be very serious about what was about to happen to the band.

We turned up in their very cool office really excited. They gave us carte blanche to choose as many albums and singles as we wanted off their various releases, which was very exciting for all of us.

They took us to a French pancake place called Obelisks where we had some lunch. The band were pretty cool and relaxed. I think the Virgin staff probably thought we were going to be crazy hard drinkers, although none of the Skids were, and drugs were never part of our life. I think they were quite surprised by how sane and moderate we were. We just wanted to know what they were going to do with us. What the plan was: what producer they wanted us to work with.

These were delicate matters because Stuart was undoubtedly the band leader and he had created our sound. The atmosphere of the band was changing because I was now writing more and more of the lyrics, so I had much more of an input in the shaping of some of the songs. But undoubtedly Stuart was the man in control and I think he was very nervous of who we were going to work with.

Over that particular lunch we spoke about various

producers, people who had worked with other bands, people who had produced albums that we really liked - which all made perfect sense, of course.

The conversation suddenly changed through talking about if we would we like to work in Scotland. The answer was 100% yes. Would we like to rehearse there? And Virgin had very cleverly thought this through, knowing that's where our identity lay. That maybe we should work with a Scottish producer, to begin with. So they asked if we were fans of The Sensational Alex Harvey Band, of which of course we were, and certainly I was in big way.

The Sensational Alex Harvey Band was one of the first bands I could ever relate to in the UK before punk rock happened. The singer, Alex Harvey, was one of the most dynamic performers I've ever seen. I found everything about them intriguing. Their music was never really my kind of music. It was a little bit more heavy rock, and sometimes almost progressive rock. Which was not to my taste, but what I loved was Alex's charisma, his dynamism, his ferociousness, and the actual terror he struck in the audience with the cartoon characters he created; these science fiction worlds that his songs inhabited, which I really, really loved.

So they talked about the producer of some of their best work, a guy called David Batchelor, whom I'd never heard of, but everybody seemed to think it was a really good idea. Our first meeting with Virgin before we put pen to paper, as they say, was a very positive meeting, they had really thought it through about who we were, what we were, and how to treat us as a work in progress. We were very rough around the edges. We were going to find it difficult to compromise with the structure of our songs. We were going to find it very difficult to be told what to do, as the whole central tenet of punk was: you determine what you wanted to do; you did it yourself. The whole DIY culture was firmly embedded in the Skids mentality. That went all the way through to things like working on our own fanzine called *Kingdom Come*, making our own record of course through No-Bad Records; and being in charge of our own destiny.

Suddenly we were being asked to share that, not with a corporation as such, but with a very cool, somewhat subversive label, Virgin, that beyond its hippie tinge, had ambitions to move into this new type of music. Of course its relationship with reggae really helped that because it made them much more credible in everybody's eyes and of course they had the Sex Pistols and... What more can you say?

We were one of their early signings and the reality of the whole process was very, very simple: We liked them, they obviously liked us. They had good ideas for where the band should go and where the band should progress to. They had come up with a fantastic idea for a producer which excited all of us. And they also understood, certainly through Stuart anyway, that pulling us away from Scotland would be a mistake. But at the same time I think they were very clear to us that in terms of our daily working schedules and getting on with stuff, and having a chance to compete with some of the most successful bands, we really needed to take the whole thing much, much more seriously than just the song writing.

I think that was a hint at the management situation. So at that moment in time it was a day of great celebration but it also was a day that ended our relationship with Pano, who'd been so kind to us, and so helpful and generous. It was really sad and tragic that we decided within hours of that day that our relationship with him was coming to an end.

In retrospect, it makes us look like we were a bunch of shits, but I think he had run out of ideas for what to do with the band, and he really couldn't take us any further. There was no doubt about that. But maybe we could have dealt with it better. We were so young. I was barely 17 years old and there I was in a record company with people from educated, privileged backgrounds, taking the words I was saying relatively seriously (and falling in love with a French Woman).

So things were changing, and very, very quickly. The decision wasn't made by me. The decision was made by the band that we had to move on.

On the way home Stuart was excited because he was going to get some money having signed a publishing deal with Virgin, as I had. Stuart's background was a little bit less impoverished than mine, but it wasn't great. Suddenly he now had an opportunity to focus on other things.

It was interesting that even on the way back to Scotland from this incredibly exciting day, I detected something in Stuart that would return many times over: this reluctance to play ball, this sense that he wanted something secure in his life. For me it was the beginning of an incredible journey. It was the moment of explosive excitement. It made perfect sense to the itinerant existence I'd always lived, so there was nothing different here. I didn't seek to have a home, a family, a wife, a mortgage, a car, and all these things. None of it made any sense to me. It didn't make any sense because at the back of my own mind was this nagging doubt that maybe I wasn't going to be around for that long because of my health which could be so dark and torturous.

But Stuart's thing was entirely different. He actually coveted these other things because he'd had an unhappy home life for different reasons. He wanted to create his own home. He wanted to create the fantasy of a nice family life, or beyond the fantasy, create a reality.

On the way home from this amazingly exciting day where the band had signed the deal with the really cool, forward-thinking record company led by Simon Draper, we felt we could do anything but I detected something... Already a twinge of Stuart's foreboding, and the way he turned his back on opportunities for seemingly no reason whatsoever. But that was only a minor thought on an extraordinary day.

Into The Valley

CHAPTER SIXTEEN

In 1978 things were really happening for the band. We had just supported the wonderful Magazine, whose debut album *Real Life* we completely loved, and became friends with the guitar player John McGeoch who later on I was to start a new band with called the Armoury Show.

John was an amazing guy, as were all the members of Magazine. The lead singer, front man Howard Devoto, had an extraordinary charisma. Very different from the way I was approaching being a front man. He was obviously very enigmatic, but at the same time had a deep mystery. I threw mystery against the wall and just got smashed into it with a physical bravado. His performance was much more inward-looking. That still worked, was still fantastic.

We played upstairs in a club called Satellite City in Glasgow, and we loved it very much. We had signed with Virgin and had found a producer who wanted to work with us in minutiae in Dunfermline. But before all that, we were asked to do something extraordinary, our first John Peel session.

Our attitude to doing a Peel session was pretty much in the spirit of both the band at the time and what John Peel was all about. Instead of doing songs that we had already written, we decided to write songs on the day and try new things and be adventurous. Rather than just do songs which had been on an early EP or for sessions we had tried to do for Virgin before working with Dave Batchelor as demos, we decided to work on new stuff. One of those songs from the first session was 'The Saints Are Coming', one of our best-known songs that's been covered by bands such as U2 and Green Day.

It was born from a crazy session down in Maida Vale at the BBC studios, with engineers who just thought we were terrible. I could tell they were more interested in progressive rock music from the likes of Emerson, Lake & Palmer, Yes, and Steve Hillage. They weren't very keen on this avant-garde punk art crap that we were barking out at them. But we had great fun doing it.

We were slightly disappointed as Peel didn't come to the sessions. We thought we'd get to meet him. But it was really amazing fun and liberating to participate in the sessions. It also gave Stuart and I an opportunity to push things in a way that maybe we felt was disappearing from the band, because we were about to enter a studio environment with a professional producer with a track record, who was himself a very good musician. This was a more anarchic individualistic approach, which had its own crazy eccentricities, that would not be approved of by our new record company or producer.

It was a last call really for that mad approach we had to song writing, where we didn't really care about things like choruses and refrains and middle eights. That was all part of traditional rock 'n' roll, which we had obviously turned our back on. Or so we thought.

It was a great experience, doing the first Peel session, despite the lack of love from the BBC engineers. It was even more exciting hearing that session go out, I think, on a cold, wet Wednesday night when we were back in Scotland. Listening to Peel as we always did and hearing that session go out, which had a Jamaican dub reggae element to it which John Peel had introduced us to, it was so exciting to hear ourselves on the radio doing something new and original and brave. We always loved some of the recordings that were made in London and we had a great affection for that type of music and applied it to our own crazy metallic punk. It had a resonance, and it worked.

Little did we know that Dave Batchelor was coming into the rehearsal studios with us in Scotland to really try and rip a bit of that out of us for all the right reasons, he thought.

The sessions with Dave Batchelor at the beginning were really interesting. We recorded our first single for Virgin with him. It was called 'Sweet Suburbia' which is probably the last of the songs that Stuart wrote that became the main releases in single terms. He had started to write more adventurous lyrics. He said that I pushed him, which I can't really recall. But he certainly had moved on from his more social commentary into something a little bit more surreal. But he had maintained his ability to create very sweet melodic choruses and guitar lines, which worked to a degree. It wasn't one of our best songs I don't think. It was very twee and quite sweet and it didn't really capture the essence of what the band was about.

The real songs that came from the sessions were the *Wide Open* EP, which had taken some of the songs we'd worked on in the Peel session in fact and advanced upon them. That was 'The Saints Are Coming', and that's really when Dave Batchelor got a hold of what the band was about and started to give it structure and a much more formal identity. If you hear the version from the Peel session of 'The Saints Are Coming' and then you hear the actual version that was released, the version that we still play to this day, they're almost completely different songs. I think they have got the same dynamic but they have a very, very different approach. The Dave Batchelor version was the first sign of us going in the direction of Stuart's great melodies and using my anthemic choruses in a way that was commercial, that would connect with people.

One of the most famous of all Skids songs from that first set of recordings that would become our debut album *Scared to Dance* was of course 'Into The Valley'. Originally when I brought those lyrics to the table the song was called 'Depersonalised'. Now that is not exactly a catchy title. The song was pulled, shifted and twisted into different directions — taken away from the artsy version of what the song was originally, and was given a much more anthemic punchy feel which is the song we know today.

That particular session working on 'Into The Valley' was particularly instructive about where the band was at. Because the sessions were going pretty well, we were being allowed to continue with some of the more crazy songs we had written like 'Scale', 'Zit', 'Six Times' and 'Integral Plot'. But the focus was on the more commercial songs, no doubt about it.

I could feel Stuart's frustration with Dave Batchelor, with overplaying the guitar lines and overplaying the commercial element and leaving behind the edginess. Which you can see on our first ever *Top of the Pops* appearance, which was for 'The Saints Are Coming' and it's really edgy. That performance has got a ferociousness about it that came from a whole array of different places. Stemming from the fact that we didn't really want to be on *Top of the Pops* because we thought it was a show where you sold out, which was idiotic of course because it was the most watched television programme in the country. To be on it gave you access to millions and millions of people who might otherwise never have heard of you.

But that performance has got a real edge and dynamic quality. It's almost like us trying to grasp back into the world of this song as it was first written, where it was much more aggressive and had a violent edge. Before it became the commercial song we know today. So these were conundrums that were playing in Stuart's head, and I think I could feel a frustration coming from him — that the band that he had created and the direction that he wanted the band to go in had hit a brick wall and was now being pulled in a completely different direction. And it was into a route that he couldn't approve of.

Then that Christmas, 1978, as the recording sessions with David were nearly coming to an end, Adamson decided to walk out on the band. This was the first proper walk out from him. He had certainly indicated in conversations with me that he was unhappy and he might just give it up, and I kept him there. But now that he was involved in a relationship with his girlfriend and soon-to-be wife Sandra, he just wanted to be home. We were recording in the Townhouse Studios in London, and he was deeply unhappy with the way the songs were being pulled with the embellishments and extra guitar lines that were not in the spirit of what the Skids were supposed to be about.

He didn't really want to be doing so many guitar overdubs, because he wanted to feel that the songs that we put onto the record could be played live to an audience, and that we wouldn't need to add other instruments to the band and keep it as a four piece.

So he basically walked out. He felt disillusioned, hurt, and cheated. It was incredibly difficult for us, because we had also seen Stuart take the money from getting a publishing deal and being able to spend that money on things that the other members of the band couldn't do to have a slightly better life. Yet he seemed to be the one who was the unhappiest.

It was difficult for all of us to really understand the depth of his unhappiness. I believe at the time he wanted to write an open letter to the music industry at large, just to say this is a world of hypocrisy and it's fake and he didn't want to be in a world of fakery. He wanted to retain artistic control and have a romantic view of how his music should be made and received.

That was insane. Just when we were at the peak of our powers as a bunch of young guys in a studio making our first album, moulding them into songs that would become enormous hit singles, Stuart walked out on us.

CHAPTER SEVENTEEN

Scared to Dance is an album that many people still hold very dearly, and respect very highly. It was an album that, at the time, was felt to be a little uneven. It had the commercial elements in there... the songs like 'Into the Valley', of course, which would go on to become hits. But, it also had really strange songs which were much more edgy and experimental. I think, there was always an artsy side to the Skids, which never left us. That probably came more from me than any of the other members. But when we were sitting working on these projects back in Dunfermline, I think Stuart enjoyed the fact that there was something unique about what we were doing.

Songs like 'Scale' and 'Six Times' were discordant and they had very peculiar structures. Even David Batchelor, who had a commercial ear, couldn't really fathom some of those songs and couldn't quite work them into more obvious commercial products. Actually, we didn't want him to. I think we really did stand tall when it came to those songs because we were very proud of them.

It's strange now to look back on the lyrics and try and work out what they were about. When I look at the lyrics to 'Six Times' now I remember what I was writing about, I was writing about masturbation and loneliness, and the two things have a connection. I placed the context of the stories in a theatrical setting. "I shot the stage six times before you came."

Then it goes into a really hard guitar line. Bum-buh-bum-buh-bum. Which gives the song a vibration which is definitely the right connection with the lyrical content. That was one of the beautiful things about working with Stuart. The two of us just sitting together and writing in the quiet of a front room somewhere and we just got on with it. I would vaguely explain what they were about, if they were overly obscure or abstract, and he would get it straight away.

Sometimes I did offer to make them a little bit more obvious and he said, "no, why? That's what you like to write, that's your style of writing, that's how you connect with words, you love words like I love music, do it." So, it's interesting you see the breakdown of the song. You have songs which have a militaristic feel, 'Melancholy Soldiers', 'Calling the Tune', 'Into the Valley', 'The Saints are Coming'. There's a common thread through those songs which deals with young people being taken from the security of their communities and their home-life and then thrust into some terrible battle zones.

The battle zone that was prevalent in all of our minds at the time was, of course, Northern Ireland. Something we all had an opinion on because the sectarian divide, although it wasn't so prevalent in the east of Scotland as the west of Scotland, still existed. The catholic community seemed to hold tight together, as did the larger, and more dominant, protestant one.

One of the great things about the Skids was that we came from both sides of that divide. We found the violence in Northern Ireland repugnant. The indiscriminate murders, the bombings, the kneecappings, the tar-and-feathering. It was so shocking to see that this was just a few miles away from people who listened to the same music as we did or read the same books and newspapers, but were hellbent on this annihilation.

I started to reflect on two things. One was a combination of my love of reading the World War I poets. Then, looking at the distress on people from the community in the central Fife mining villages I lived in, who were coming home from serving time in Northern Ireland. There was no doubt that they had changed. Their demeanour had changed, their outlook had changed, and ones who hadn't gone out as bigots certainly returned as bigots.

Most of the people who were joining the army who were my age were from the protestant community. The equivalent members of the catholic community were being navigated away from joining because they knew they would be sent to Northern Ireland and to be a young catholic soldier in one of the Scottish regiments over there would make you a number one target from both sides. So, it was something that was to be avoided. Strangely it was always a desire of mine, before this love of music and words became the direction for my life. I actually thought that maybe the army would be a place where I would find some friendship and camaraderie. But, of course, I would never have been accepted because of my health condition.

But, these songs, 'Melancholy Soldiers', more literally 'Calling the Tune', and 'The Saints Are Coming', deal with these very issues of young people desperate for a job, and their identity, and some pride. Rather than just being thrown on the scrap heap at such an early age they joined the army, got some discipline from that, earned the wage and then suddenly, they were sent into hardened battle zones, because that's what Belfast was, and Derry, and a lot of the outlying areas. Certainly, around the border between the south and the north. These were hugely violent places for a young person to be thrown into.

So, they came back changed and 'Into the Valley'. 'Depersonalised', didn't capture that, but it did capture the sense of somebody going into the battle with a sense of purpose and returning absolutely distraught and destroyed, and changed. So, essentially, the overlying theme of these songs was all about change.

The other songs on *Scared to Dance* have a slightly different feel, less literal, a little bit more abstract, but they all deal with paranoia.

'Integral Plot' is essentially at the top of that particular list. 'Six Times' falls into the same category as does 'Scale'. Songs about not fitting in, feeling alienated, feeling isolated, feeling that the world's against you. But, this was the 1970s and that's how people felt. People our age felt like the world had turned its back on us. It was difficult to get a job other than in the obvious industrial areas like going down a mine or joining the British Army. The idea that people from our background could express themselves through art, culture, and music was an obscenity, not just to the more rarefied, bourgeois world which controlled, and still does control the arts, but actually the communities we came from.

The idea that you would waste your time sitting in a back room writing songs, you were seen as a layabout, as somebody who wasn't contributing to the more traditional route that these communities took. So, it was a lose-lose situation really, to be a creative person who actually sought to find their identity through that. This is something I'd seen with Francis, who was just so different from everybody else. Even the way he looked and dressed, and the music he listened to, his general behaviour, the way he spoke and what he spoke about, did not fit the norm and if you didn't fit the norm in these communities then you were seen as somebody who was trying to stand out for all the wrong reasons, or you had some obvious mental health issue.

So, these were things you were up against and, a lot of those songs actually deal with the alienation of coming from that background and feeling, how do you make a move into the arts when the arts are completely controlled by the class system? Which was fairly well structured in British society. The kind of communities that we came from, the idea of talking about the arts, or participating in the arts, was absolutely never discussed and never talked about, because it just didn't happen.

At the same time as being aware of this social exclusion I'd started to read books by Jean-Paul Sartre. *The Age of Reason* trilogy, which dealt with exactly that, an existential gloom, a sense of isolation and loss. Put that together with my own sickness, even though I felt energised by the music there was a weariness in taking on this battle every day. Because you started the day as a loser and you had to fight from that position. You didn't start the day as a winner, you're already lost, you had to just make gains, and you had to be brave about that.

I think the lyrical content of *Scared to Dance* attempts to capture that particular mood. The sleeve was designed by Russell Mills, a very well-known artist at the time. He had done all the Brian Eno ambient sleeves and I really liked his work. I went to meet him where he lived in a little mews in Camden Town to discuss the sleeve. We talked about the books I was reading, and the idea of the café society world where people discussed embracing gloom and self-destruction, because we still lived at the height of the Cold War. These were the quite depressing themes that we talked about.

So, we ended up with this sleeve of a person sitting in a corner in a marble bar, which could be from the Weimar era in Berlin, or Paris in the 1930s, sitting alone, staring at a world passing him by, and he was trying to work out really is it worth trying to jump on. Because he looked like he'd already jumped off. I think that's really where we were, or certainly where I was, at that moment in time. Do you jump on and have a go? Or do you jump off before you get found out.

So, the sleeve, in many ways, was an encapsulation of the mood of the songs — the general sense of existential gloom that was surrounding us and how we, as young men, responded to that. I'm immensely proud of the cover, it really captured what we were about. We even had the audacity to put a Jean-Paul Sartre quote on the back.

I think we got absolutely derided for doing that, but who cares? It was our album, our sleeve, our identity, so we did what we wanted to do. It was met with a quote from a guy called Ronnie Gurr. Ronnie was a local journalist in Edinburgh who we had met very early on in the scene in the east of Scotland. He was a pretty switched-on guy. He had his own fanzine called *Hanging Around*. He loved music and was at the heart of the Edinburgh scene. He interviewed most of the bands that came to Scotland, and he went south to watch bands like we did. He was becoming very well-known as the figurehead go-to guy in Scotland who understood what was happening and where.

We'd meet him a lot. At Stranglers and Buzzcocks gigs, on the White Riot Tour and hang out with them. He was very, very supportive of the band and he was very close to us. I think he even travelled down to London on the day that we signed to Virgin. We've got a quote from him on the back of it about the fact that we were wrapped up in our own classic rock 'n' roll paranoia. Which was absolutely true, because we felt the world was against us, we felt our music was the most important thing but nobody understood it, and nobody understood what we were trying to do. We took everything to heart, took everything so personally.

So, we had this amazing mixture of guts and bravery to just go and do it, but at the same time this terror of the world beyond us and what actually that meant in terms of mutually assured annihilation with the possibility of nuclear destruction, which faced us as on a daily basis. I'm sure in many ways that informed our songs and attitude as one of the many layers of what punk represented. That it was very inherently in there somewhere.

This was the world we were in, and *Scared to Dance* represented that world as well as we could have possibly done at that point in time.

I think it's an uneven album but, this was a classic period for people who still wanted to make an album that had a beginning, and a middle, and an end, which seems to have disappeared now. People are really just interested in one big song and then everything else seems to be a filler. Whereas we actually attacked our album with care, love, and attention. Even to this day, with the recently released *Burning Cities*, that project was attacked with absolutely the same care and attention to the fact that there had to be a consistency through the album. There had to be different dynamicsat play, and a sense of identity coming through the music. I think we achieved that, and certainly *Scared to Dance* showed a band rich in artistic ambition but completely clouded with paranoia.

Into The Valley

CHAPTER EIGHTEEN

After the completion of *Scared to Dance* and the finalising of the art work, the elephant in the room was still how to deal with Adamson's departure. We had hidden this as much as we could from Virgin, who thought he had gone because someone had been ill in his family. As usual it was down to me to arrange to meet up with him and talk it through. These meetings were always strange affairs. He always acted as if nothing had happened and that we had done nothing other than have a short break.

I would ask if he was okay and he would talk about getting together to write new songs. No drama. It was almost as if he couldn't bear real confrontation, maybe he was nervous of my more aggressive side. There was no discussion about some of the guitar overdubs having been done by the sound engineer in the studio. No discussion about his emotional stability. No sense of where the anger came from and where it had gone. This was something that would run parallel to everything we did as the Skids until we no longer existed as a writing partnership. Basically by the end I just couldn't be arsed constantly running back to him. It was humiliating for me. But at this point in time there was so much at stake. Virgin had big plans for the band and were certain we could break big. I tried to put the Stuart Adamson disappearing act behind me and get focussed on the madness that was on the horizon. Our lives were about to change and go up a gear in a way that we could never have imagined.

The song that propelled the band and the album, *Scared to Dance*, to the top of the UK charts and made us a household name overnight was 'Into the Valley'. It had become the iconic Skids track, it's a song that a lot of people seem to have done some high kicking to at some point in time in their life or jumped around in a state of dizzy fun. For a lot of younger people, maybe around the age of 12 and 13 it was a song that may have been the first record they ever bought, so it defined them and their identity.

Not unlike the kind of music that I had got into at their age which had given me a very clear identity, be it Lou Reed or David Bowie, 'Into the Valley' was their song. But when we were preparing to release our next record there was nobody in the band that had any sense that this was going to be big. We'd, had previous attempts to get into the charts with 'The Saints are Coming' and made the lower end, but not the break- through. I remember the period of building up to the release of 'Into the Valley', just before the album came out.

It was the album that we were talking about because we were the album generation. It was all about the release of this 12" piece of magical vinyl that was exciting us the most. We hadn't really given much thought to the whole idea of 'Into the Valley' being released as a single. Even the sleeve was approached differently, we've always been very careful about them and wanted them to be like little mini bits of art but that sleeve was shot in a studio in Notting Hill by a really cool photographer called Dennis Morris.

It was a press shot for the PR division of Virgin down in Vernon Yard and Dennis was a very cool, young black guy who was friends with the Virgin gang because he took shots of a lot of the reggae acts for them. They put us in a studio on Campden Hill Road in Kensington. Dennis set up very quickly and the idea was that it was going to have this pink background which we just thought was the most ludicrous idea. We were all in a strange mood I think that day, so none of us really felt like fighting it.

He just seemed like such a nice guy. He wasn't the most talkative person, but he was a very, very sweet guy. He said that it was a nice contrast to the fact that we look like these street urchins from Scotland and quite aggressive looking.

Suddenly having something a little bit softer behind us might just give it a little bit of contrast. We thought it was idiotic, but Dennis was very gently convincing, so we went along with it and didn't argue. Even though that photo session took a very short time to do and our heart wasn't in it, Dennis convinced us it was going to be something that would get a lot of attention and be very dynamic. To us it just looked like any other young punk band sleeve. You put the band on the cover and you get the identity of the band through that.

We always wanted the identity to come through some of our ideas, so like the cover of *Scared to Dance* having such an enigmatic, mysterious quality. There's very little mystery in the cover for 'Into the Valley'. The build-up to the release of the record was not particularly exciting, we had been touring with The Stranglers which had been in itself truly magical. We had been learning a lot about performance from them because every night they delivered, no matter what state they were in.

No matter how big or small the venue was, it didn't matter, it was all about getting on that stage and delivering the goods. We had a really strong relationship with Jean-Jacques and Hugh Cornwell who were incredibly generous to us. Hugh remains my friend to this day, he's somebody who I have an amazing respect for, as I do the other members of The Stranglers. Hugh is a wise owl. I've taken council from him on many different subjects and I regard him as 100% decent human being.

We were playing with them in a mixture of college venues and small arenas. It was very exciting because every gig would've been sold out and as the support band nobody really cares much, but we started to make a dent in the tour. Halfway through that tour it broke off. I think they went to America and we were going to pick up with them again later on in the year, at which point in time we returned to Scotland.

It was a strange return for me because I felt so distant from everyone. My relationship with my family was pretty much non-existent, although I still hung out with my brothers. Francis had left Edinburgh and had gone to London and it was very difficult to find him there as he seemed to be moving around a lot so I didn't see him that often. I saw Michael and even the youngest one Brian who hung out with the band. I started to see a bit more of John, who had his own career, so he was really never around, but I never really wanted to spend any time at home.

There was still that underlying tension in the band as well with the Stuart Adamson gone missing scenario. You just felt it was in the room all the time, and that at any point this guy could just go I'm not happy with this situation, I don't really want to be in a band, I don't really feel the need to find success in this, creatively or even commercially.

The previous release of 'Sweet Suburbia' and 'The Saints are Coming' hadn't been particularly successful, it had also had mixed reviews from journalists, which definitely affected him quite badly.

I took it with a pinch of salt and I still do to this day. I found sometimes music journalists essentially were frustrated musicians themselves who wanted to be in a band. Sometimes they took out their frustrations on people who actually got up there and got on with it and raised their head above the parapet. So there was sometimes a nasty bitterness in these journalists, I'm sure that went right across the board into film and books and other forms of cultural criticism.

Stuart was definitely a guy who was constantly on the edge and this had nothing to do with drinking too much or taking drugs. It was just to do with his own darkness and there was a cloud around him all the time. He wanted to be back home, he felt more at peace and relaxed when he got back to Dunfermline, now he had this permanent relationship with Sandra, so, he had something very strong and committed to come back to, whereas I didn't.

I had started meeting other band members and people of a similar mind-set in London, I'd been hanging out with Paul Cook, the drummer from Sex Pistols and I'd met Steve Severin from Siouxsie and the Banshees. I'd been running around a lot with Rusty Egan from the Rich Kids who had his own nightclub where he DJ'd. The club was called Billy's in Soho which would then move on to Covent Garden to become the legendary New Romantic club the Blitz. So there was a lot going on and I was going to see bands every night in the various venues. I was always being invited by bands to come and see them and I was making a lot of friends, something I'd never managed to do in Scotland with the same gusto. I think it was the sense that I was in a band, I had a bit of attitude and there was a real sense of camaraderie and friendship. Even though Siouxsie and the Banshees' music was very different from what the Skids were doing, they seemed to take me under their wing without being judgemental about my music. I was always a Banshees fan, I don't think they were such big Skids fans, although Severin was always very supportive. I had all these new connections and was suddenly hanging out at things that I'd never thought about doing. Like going to see some weird, strange theatre events at the ICA or going to art exhibitions in the various galleries around London. I was being invited to perform in clubs by people who were not just musicians, but poets and performers and actors. The London thing really excited me. Just going down to King's Road and getting some clothes was always a magical experience, or hanging out in Kensington High Street at the Kensington Market.

I loved it there, a mixture of punk and hippie sensibilities and down in the basement a mixture of little food cafés and barber shops. It was really exciting to be in amongst it. I got a sense of the DIY culture of punk in action where young people were just getting on with it, starting their own little shops or their own bookshops, fashion shops, barber shops or doing club nights, it just had an energy that really meant a lot to me.

Then we released 'Into the Valley' on the back of all this sense of tension and excitement. I don't think we were aware that our fan base had grown to be quite as big and it was quite a surprise that the record went so high into the charts and we were on *Top of the Pops*. I think that probably happened because we played live a lot. We were constantly out and about doing stuff. We'd been picking up a lot of fans from playing support with big bands, such as The Stranglers, The Buzzcocks or The Clash.

It was a strange day when we arrived at the BBC Studios. They wanted to cover us in makeup and we absolutely wouldn't allow that. Then there was a bit of a fight about it because these very posh BBC people demanded that we had something on to take the shine off our face, so we had to compromise with that.

Then the same old thing with Stuart, should we be doing a show like *Top of the Pops*? A lot of the other acts on that particular evening were ridiculous stuff that we didn't like. So we felt our usual paranoia and intense rage at the world when we were asked to come up and do a rehearsal. At that point in time I felt really sick, like I was going to have one of my epileptic seizures.

I told Stuart and he immediately said to the BBC people, he's not well, I don't think we can do a rehearsal, but we'll just have to do it without him. So the general compromise that was found was that I would stand in position if I could and they would get all the camera angles done and get ready for the performance later in the evening when the creepy DJs appear to introduce us etc.

We went back to the dressing room, the other guys I think went out for a wander around Shepherd's Bush, which was quite a rough and tumble area at the time, and I just stayed in the dressing room on my own in the BBC Centre. It was a miserable place in the vaults of the basement with no natural light, horrible strips of lighting, like little prison cells. I felt really terrible, that I couldn't possibly go on and do this, but nearer the time, around 7:00, the band were back and, Stuart asked me how I felt. I was honest with him, I said "I feel terrible, but we're only going to get one crack at this tonight because I'm only going to be able to do it once, let's just go for it."

The general feeling was that we got ourselves pumped up because it was only going to be a one-off performance. With lots of the other performances on *Top of the Pops* they did one, sometimes two, even three, maybe even four performances so they got all the varied camera angles. It was shot the night before it went out, on the Wednesday, so they had time to edit it all together. So we got ourselves in position on the stage and I said to Stuart, "let's just go for it, let's just go mad because we're not going to be able to do this again, I feel so terrible."

The director of the show had not prepared for me moving around because at the rehearsal I hadn't done anything, I just stood at the microphone. But suddenly when the music kicked in we just exploded, like we do on stage, into this physical powerhouse, diving around the stage, embracing the song, embracing the volley and thunder of the music — and absolutely vomiting the lyrics out as I did some massive high kicks. It was hugely problematic for the production and camera team because they hadn't been aware that this was going to happen.

After we finished the performance they said "oh, we weren't expecting that, we need to do it again" and that's when Stuart just said "no, he's not well enough, that's it. If it doesn't work, it doesn't work, don't use it, but we can't do it again." So they had to use the one performance I was able to do. It was strange because we got back to Scotland the next day and we had been through the *Top of the Pops* experience before, so our expectations were pretty low.

Even though it was the biggest television show, or certainly the biggest music show, of that era, watched by most of the country, it was still possible to go on and fail, because we had with 'The Saints are Coming'. So on that Thursday night we were introduced and it was just hilarious to watch the band, preparing to deliver the song.

I was wearing this atrocious leopard skin jacket, I looked like an idiot, but I was so grey and sick, and we just exploded into life — the BBC obviously had used the one take. It was quite messy, but they used the whole thing. I remember the response of my parents because I watched it at their place and they were saying, "what the hell happened there? That was embarrassing, that was absolutely idiotic." I went "oh, fair enough, I actually quite liked it, I thought it was really funny." We were just crazy and it actually caught the spirit of The Skids, and I slept on it and didn't think anything of it.

I knew the next day something was up because we went to rehearsal in the usual place and there was hundreds of young people waiting outside. I often arrived earlier than the other guys so I could just sit and come up with some new lyrics. There were all these young people there between the ages of 12 and 17 who just wanted to talk about this insane performance on *Top of the Pops* the previous night. It was really sweet and great fun chatting to them all, but they really were affected by it. By the time the other guys in the band arrived we just knew something had happened and everything had changed for the band.

When we walked to town for instance, and went to a café, people were shouting out of their car windows at us. I'm not sure it was nice things, but they were shouting at us anyway. When we walked down the street people were pointing at us. Again people, where we came from, weren't very shy of coming forward. So they were giving us their view of our performance on *Top of Pops* the previous night, which was not entirely favourable I might add. It had made this impression on people, which was I think quite threatening. Young people just loved it, but older people definitely seemed threatened by it.

When we went back on tour and started playing again with The Stranglers we knew immediately everything had changed. That's when we could really tell because that tour was about them, it wasn't about us. At previous gigs a lot of

Into The Valley

the audience didn't come in to watch us, they'd be in the bar or they hadn't even arrived. But now we'd go on stage and it would be the same audience waiting for us to play as for The Stranglers, it was full. They really were attentive to what we were doing and we got an amazing response.

A support band was never meant to go on and do an encore, but The Stranglers were very cool and they actually allowed us to do an encore and enjoy this new success. 'Into the Valley' just kept on going up and up the charts until it got into the top ten and we were back on *Top of the Pops*. We still did the same ferocious performance that was completely uncompromising.

Essentially the performance was all about four people who were very intense who were full of a physicality and madness, but actually we were having a lot of fun and our friendship really comes over in those performances. Stuart was much more relaxed, suddenly all his frustration with the music industry and with where we were headed changed because we had done something that really connected with people. Literally overnight our worlds changed and we were a band who people wanted to see on their own. From being a support act to The Stranglers which was magic, we were being offered big gigs, for the first time as the Skids — supporting nobody and just getting on with it.

That was terrifying because we had never really played big venues as a headline act, but now it was an impossibility to hide away from that. That's really what 'Into the Valley' did to all of us — it brought us into a place where we could no longer hide behind our posturing, behind our attitudes, behind our fear of failure. We were no longer a failure, we were a success, commercially at least. Creatively we had a long way to go, but suddenly people were interested in us, right across the board people knew who we were. They knew from that performance on *Top of the Pops* that there was a new band in town and younger people specifically adopted us as their band.

That's just something that seems to have never gone away because we went back out on tour recently with *Burning Cities*, which was released in January 2018. Those young people who were caught in that storming performance of 'Into the Valley', who may have been 10, 11, 12, 13 who couldn't get into some of the venues to see us have now come along to see us at last, hopefully we haven't disappointed them, obviously Stuart Adamson is no longer with us sadly. The people who come to the shows talk about that moment when they watched these crazy guys from Scotland getting up on that stage and just driving their song through the television straight at them and it was a defining moment for them and it was a defining moment for us.

Into The Valley

CHAPTER NINETEEN

After the incredible success of 'Into The Valley' and the release of *Scared To Dance*, which pushed it into the UK top ten, the Skids world had undoubtedly changed. Everything seemed to move so quickly, it was difficult to understand where we were headed. Everybody wanted to talk to us, newspapers, magazines, radio shows. You just walked down the street and people would stop you and have a conversation. Television in those days was so powerful that it made you feel familiar to people, in a way that they felt they knew you or they wanted to have a conversation with you. Undoubtedly, our world of an insular band, wrapped up in our own ideas about our own paranoia had changed. It felt like we were no longer in charge of our own destiny. It seemed we were now owned by the world around us. It was an extraordinary shift and it happened at a pace that we could never have imagined. It happened so quickly that we didn't really find the tools to deal with it. No one was giving us the proper advice. The management we had at the time was Sandy Muir, the guy who had the record store and put out our first EP, *Charles*. But, he wasn't equipped to deal with this. He was just a guy who owned a small record store in a small town.

He hadn't a clue what was going on. Within the band there developed a strange dynamic of Stuart and myself, and Bill and Tom. The rhythm section started to feel slightly put out that all of the interviews were being done by Stuart and I. Because we had a publishing deal and had received a little bit of money, they started to feel excluded from what was going on and that definitely left a bad taste in their mouth. This is a common dynamic in bands, but we weren't to know that at the time. You felt that anything could happen on any given day.

Even though this was a world without social media, without mobile phones or the Internet, a much more analogue world, in the context of the speed of things our lives had dramatically shifted. We were in a different gear now and the general reaction to us was a mixture of pride, for sure — adulation from young people and bitterness from a lot of other older people. People didn't like the fact that we were being successful. I think that was part of the Scottish psyche, at the time that success was greeted with disdain.

A lot of people felt that I was an attention-seeker and that I was grasping for some position and that, obviously, I held myself in some high regard. Of course, none of that is true. If they only knew the truth, that each evening I'd go back to where I was still living in Dunfermline and that I was constantly ill and had no relationship with anyone. I had no girlfriend. I was pretty much a lonely person still, even though people imagined that my life, suddenly, overnight, had become this marvellous thing, which it really hadn't.

Did I like the attention? Well, I guess. It was something that fed into my system, in a strange way. I didn't reject it. I liked talking, so I wasn't shy about the band. Suddenly, I'm being asked opinions about what's going on in the world politically; this new person arriving on the scene called Margaret Thatcher; what antipathy did I feel towards her, which was pretty enormous; and the general way that the industrial belt where I came from was coming to an end and jobs for life were a thing of the past. People were facing a dramatic change, and it was almost like Stuart's song 'Charles' had become a prophecy of what was now happening to people. Automation was coming in, traditional skills were no longer required and Britain was moving towards becoming a global service industry and financial sector and moving away from industrialisation and manufacturing. These were big changes.

People were asking my opinion about these things. I'm seventeen years old and people want to know where I stand politically, which was easy enough. But, then, to actually break it down and talk coherently about it... you've had this enormously successful record, and people really feel absolutely secure that you must know what you're talking about. Of course, I didn't. I was just as naïve and as foolish and idiotic as any other seventeen year old.

But, seventeen for us, then, meant you were a man. You had to grow up so fast that you almost felt, because of the band, that those formative years of being a teenager and moving into adulthood had been ripped away. Because we had been working so hard as performers that almost the performance side of you starts to take over and the real you, whoever that is and whatever that was, starts to slink into the shadows and you start to create a character. You start to almost add little bits as you go along, little flourishes of who this person is and make it up as you go along.

There's a wonderful expression by the French artist, Jean Cocteau, "the lie that tells the truth". That's true in this case, where you start to create a mythical sense of yourself to make yourself a little bit more interesting to people. But, actually, invariably, that becomes the truth. It becomes the truth about who you are because you don't really know who

Into The Valley

you are. You don't really know what you're supposed to be or what you might have been in other circumstances. You're just in this strange, almost mythical world where people want a part of you. At that moment in time, we had been doing a small tour and we finished it headlining in Dunfermline, at the Kinema Ballroom, which was a legendary venue.

We had played there with The Clash of course, as the opening act. But, we had never headlined. There we were, at the peak of our early success, and we were playing a night at the ballroom. One of the most exciting things I remember about playing that venue was seeing busloads of people coming from outlying areas, like Kirkcaldy and Lochgelly and all the small mining villages. They were bringing busloads of people in to see the local band who had become a sensation overnight with 'Into The Valley'. It was an amazing gig. I remember going on stage and I had slicked my hair back with gel and was just loving the performance.

Stuart was flying through the air in one direction, I was flying through the air in another direction. There was a sense of joy in the band. Stuart was always happiest when he was on home turf. He knew, at the end of the gig, he would be with Sandra. He knew he would be amongst friends and he was much calmer and easier to be around and work with in these circumstances. I was spinning up into the air and landing as he took off. It was pretty magical stuff.

I actually went back to stay at my parents' house that night and slept on their sofa. When I woke up in the morning, I couldn't open my eyes. The gel had run into my eyes with the sweat and had glued them together. I was rushed to hospital where they had to operate to unclench my eyes and there was an absolute terror that I had blinded myself. Luckily, I was fine. It couldn't take away the triumph of the previous evening. It was just one of those magical nights where everything came together and there was a sense of joy in the air, a sense of pride and all the anxieties and stupidity and idiocies of the band had been put aside for this one particular night.

When my eyesight came back into play, we started to talk about our next record. We spoke about various producers and I had suggested we use Bill Nelson of Be Bop Deluxe, one of Stuart's heroes. He was an amazing guitar player. Be Bop Deluxe had recently split and Nelson had started his new project, Red Noise. I thought it might be a way of keeping Stuart happy, unlike the last experience on *Scared To Dance* where he was pulled away into a studio he didn't want to be in, with a producer he didn't seem to be happy with. But, this time, he'd be working with one of his heroes, so he was going to learn a lot from him. It was a dream come true for him. Also, Bill Nelson had dropped the very thing that everybody loved about him, being this guitar hero, and become a much more interesting artist with Red Noise. I thought, maybe he could do something similar for the Skids. We had created the sound, now it was time to evolve it.

Virgin Records didn't love the idea, but didn't hate it either. So, they sent us off to try and work with Bill on a couple of new songs and Bill was going to come and work with us in Dunfermline.

He lived in Yorkshire and had come along to see us when we had played near his home in the outlying area of Wakefield. I got the feeling at the time that the Skids were not the sort of band that he was listening to. There were other things happening using a synthetic sound and a lot of the influence of German music. Simple Minds from Scotland, for example, were beginning to make a bit of noise. Quite rightly, because they were really good and I think Bill was more interested in what they were about. We were also talking about Joy Division led by the wonderful Ian Curtis and he thought they were pushing music in another direction, too. Although, their album, *Unknown Pleasures,* had not been released at that stage, there was a sense they were going to be something special.

These were the bands Bill was talking about. He was just saying, maybe you guys could push your sound a little bit further, which I thought was really exciting. I could feel hesitancy from Stuart, but we went in and we worked on some material and the key track we worked on was 'Masquerade', which, to this day, remains one of my favourite Skids' songs. It's one of my favourite lyrics. I'd written this two-voice lyric almost like a chant and answer type thing, almost something you'd hear on a parade ground; it was an anti-war statement about the absolute lunacy and idiocy of battle and going to war.

I'd been looking at prints of a wonderful painting by Picasso, called *Guernica*, and that really influenced the song. I wanted to call it 'Guernica', but, again, not the most catchy or commercial title. But, I actually managed to get the name Guernica in the lyrics, which came to me very quickly and Bill really loved them. I remember that it was the first time anybody other than Stuart had given me a massive thumbs up about the style of my writing. I'd been given quite a hard time from critics with the release of 'Into The Valley' and *Scared To Dance*. They felt my lyrics were almost too stylised, too obtuse, and abstract, and that they were pretentious, which was quite hurtful. But, que sera. If you put your head above the parapet, you're going to get it and I definitely got it.

But, with 'Masquerade', I didn't change. I stuck with it. The lyrics were written in Dunfermline Carnegie Library. I'd go in there and sit because it was quiet, warm and full of atmosphere, which I really loved. I'm very proud of the fact that I used that wonderful facility which, to this day, still exists and is still an amazing space and location for people to use.

I knew what I wanted to write about and I knew I wanted the chorus to have that anthemic feel that could be sung along with easily. Stuart and I talked a bit about what the themes were and he started playing this amazing guitar line which was really edgy and fierce, and it was magical. Nelson heard it and said, well, we've almost got it. He made some suggestions with the drums and we brought in a synthesiser which everybody was horrified by. What the hell are the Skids doing with a synthesiser? But, it gave it a dance beat that the song wouldn't have had otherwise. He used these sequencer patterns, which he programmed, that really gave the song an amazing boost and elevated it to a wonderful position that it might not have had — a combination of that synth layer and Stuart's really tough, edgy guitar lines, with that amazing guitar break and melody, combining with the chant and answer style of the vocals in the verses... Then, you suddenly go to this really quite sweet but melodic chorus, "holy to the high masquerade, fanfares in the sky masquerade."

It just felt like it worked and when we got into the recording studio and worked with Bill, it really went well. Stuart was happy. He loved working with Bill, who was taking his guitar playing into a new place and he also liked the notion of adding these synthetic layers which moved our sound on.

So, all the things I was slightly worried about with Stuart weren't there. He was really quite excited by this and he felt we were with the right man to move the band along, so, it really felt really good.

Into The Valley

At this point in time, I had decided to move into a flat just off the King's Road, down the bottom end at World's End, with some people I had met, just to get a sense of what it might be like to live in London. I think that horrified Stuart and Bill (Simpson). The idea that I could go as far away as London and how the hell was that going to work for the band. But, I just really wanted to try it. So, between recording 'Masquerade' and then starting to prepare the songs for what would become *Days In Europa*, I had made a big geographical shift. I really needed it for myself. My world was imploding a little bit, on a personal level and I just needed something else, another edge, another thing to give me that creative push. I just felt London was so exciting and had a wow factor. I was meeting people my own age with similar ambitions and energy which was just so magical.

Having made the decision to move to London, in many ways, even though the band was working really nicely and we'd got this situation with the producer really worked out and Stuart was happy, I threw a cog in the wheels by suddenly pushing myself four hundred miles away from the other guys. No one had ever done that in our small world. We had all stuck together and we were living out of each other's pockets.

Stuart, especially, didn't understand that, but it was clear to me, he had a girlfriend who he spent all his time with, I didn't socialise with him anymore because he spent all his time with her. Of course, that's what you would do, but I needed more and I had nothing in Dunfermline. No emotional life and it was very slow and provincial at that time (its got a hell of a lot better) so, the decision I made was very selfish, I guess. But, if I hadn't made it, I think I would've gone insane.

CHAPTER TWENTY

The rehearsals for the recording of *Days in Europa* were held in Dunfermline in the same small garage space where we had been working from the very beginning. Although the band's stature had risen and our success had passed beyond any level we could ever have imagined, we still seemed to be pretty much in the same place. We didn't actually have any money even though we had sold a lot of records.

This issue with the publishing deal had rankled Tom and Bill to a degree that Tom felt the band had become something he didn't really want to be part of anymore. He much preferred small town life and would have preferred to play in a pub band, so he left.

It was no great loss because he wasn't the greatest drummer in the world although he had a lot of energy. Stuart used to write all his parts for him. To advance our music further, I think we needed to go up a little anyway. It was a shame to lose him as a personality because he was great fun to have around, but I think his time in the Skids had naturally come to an end.

I had become friends with Rusty Egan. His band the Rich Kids which he had put together with Glen Matlock, formerly of the Sex Pistols, along with Midge Ure had a brief lifespan. It hadn't really worked the way they had imagined. They came across as just wanting to be pop stars, which was pretty much against the punk ethos.

Rusty was a good drummer and he was switched on to where things were headed musically. The only problem with him was he had a mouth that never stopped. He was a motormouth. He had opinions about everything. About what the band should be doing, what they should be wearing. Our experiences, he kept on telling us, were so limited to living in a small town and not advancing beyond that. He really got under the skin of the other members of the band, but he was a good drummer.

I had been staying with him a lot in London in his Notting Hill Gate flat which he shared with Steve Strange who became better known as the front person for The Blitz and Visage.

Rusty came up to Dunfermline to start rehearsing with us, which was strange because he did look like an alien had landed in Dunfermline. He didn't really fit into the local environment. Rusty didn't drink alcohol or take drugs. Not that people in Dunfermline necessarily took drugs, but they certainly drank a lot. Rusty really wasn't interested in that kind of thing.

He would come out with us into the various bars, and he nearly got in a fight every single night. People just wanted to beat him up because of his attitude and the way he dressed. I always protected Rusty physically from harm because I felt he was a statement in his own right. He was wearing clothes from a shop called PX in Covent Garden.

At that time Covent Garden was badly run-down. It was just after the fruit markets had moved over to South London and the place was not the glamorous Covent Garden that it is today. In the midst of this was a really amazing shop called PX where the main designer in there, Helen, was creating these almost sci-fi clothes. Rusty and Steve Strange were some of the first people to wear them. He encouraged me to start wearing those clothes. So if there is anybody to blame for the terrible clothes that I wore during *Days in Europa*, it was undoubtedly Rusty Egan!

The one thing we did share together was a great love of David Bowie so we had that to share, at least. But he never really understood small town politics. He was a London boy through and through. He was a little bit patronising about small town life, which of course didn't go down well with the other guys.

The rehearsals happened every day. Everyone was excited that Bill Nelson was going to produce the album; including Virgin because 'Masquerade' had been a hit and people loved the sound of it. It felt like we had moved on from 'Into the Valley' and had created another anthem of a kind, but it felt fresher.

Stuart's guitar playing had evolved to another level. My lyrics were my lyrics; I was never going to change that. But I still managed to hook people in with the choruses which gave me free reign to do what I wanted with the verses.

It felt to me like we had turned a page. This was new even though everything was the same. As in we hadn't advanced any further financially, but creatively, we sensed we were on the move. Having Nelson at the helm really seemed to be a provocative idea. He was going to push us away from our punk roots into making our sound a little bit more sophisticated, possibly into using more electronic instruments such as keyboards.

It felt like a really exciting moment. We were talking to him about new ideas. I talked to him constantly about the lyrics that I was writing. He was so supportive. He said, don't change things if people don't understand them, let them catch up, don't go backwards for them. It was advice that would stay with me to this day. Musically, he started to pull the songs apart, make them less cluttered with guitar riffs and give them more space. The first tunes that came out of those rehearsals in Dunfermline were songs like 'Working for the Yankee Dollar', which was another anti-war song, about the horror of what people had been through from the First World War through the Second World War and Vietnam.

At that point in time in cinema history, there was a whole array of revisionist films being released from the USA about the Vietnam Conflict. They were movies that had a different sensibility. They weren't blood-and- thunder movies. They were wrapped up in a sadness that ordinary people were sucked into a conflict in the jungles of Vietnam and paid the price.

'Working for the Yankee Dollar' in many ways was a reflection of those kinds of films that were prevalent during that period which really caught the movie-going public's imagination and were very critical of American intervention in Southeast Asia.

The title track, 'The Olympian'... I say title track because the album was originally going to be called *The Olympian* but later as we progressed it obviously became *Days in Europa*... It was the next track worked on. It felt instantly like a Skids song. A big chorus, lots of chanting and a very ferocious Stuart Adamson guitar line.

Nelson moved it around a lot and gave it different qualities. Rusty's drumming is exceptional. I think Rusty's drumming on the whole album gave the Skids a much better tempo. Even songs like 'Working for the Yankee Dollar' had a dance beat rather than a punk beat. That definitely came from Rusty. That was a song that initially sounded more like it could have come from the world of the The Clash.

By the time we had finished working with Bill Nelson, Rusty had done his drum rhythm and the keyboards had been added, it became something entirely different and became the song that it is today. The influence of Bill Nelson and certainly Rusty on the album is huge.

My favourite song on the album is 'Animation'. They're the best lyrics I had ever written. They're lyrics that are about being caught in an almost suspended world where you're unable to control anything. I had been reading *The Gulag Archipelago* by Solzhenitsyn and it had a major effect on me. How people could suddenly be pulled out of their normal life and thrown into the wilderness and just be forgotten like they didn't exist anymore.

'Animation' was a reflection of that, but I wrote it almost like you were looking at a movie. I brought a lot of those Russian poster ideas into the lyrics. Labour saving days, Leisure loving days, all these lines come from those amazing Soviet posters which I still love and recently went to actually see again at an exhibition at the Tate in London. It reminded me how a lot of those lyrics on *Days in Europa* came about looking at those wonderful posters from the Soviet Revolution.

I still feel the lyrics are the best I ever wrote for the Skids. The song felt so beautiful. Stuart's guitar line was really elegant and quite hypnotic. Rusty's drumming was inspired. He did this almost military roll underneath it which gave the song a repetitive loop feel which still feels modern when we play it live to this day. We always play 'Animation', first and foremost because it's my favourite Skids song. But secondly, it just seems to evolve. It has got an elegance that has never waned.

It's stood the test of time.

So the rehearsal period with these songs and this new combination of people working seemed to be going really well. Rusty amongst a group is combustible because he gets your back up very quickly. He was incredibly patronising about us and where we came from which is something we were deeply proud of and he had misunderstood that. He just saw it as a rural backwater where people were quite primitive and they didn't have the big city ideas and elegance of people like himself. But that was his own conflation of who he thought he was and the scene that he was in back in London.

But at the same time, I think he had a sneaking regard for what we were doing with the album. He knew that we were a band who were trying to progress. We were trying to make our songs feel like they were moving beyond the punk movement. Keeping the spirit, of course, but moving into something even a little bit more European. That's where of course we started to think about the title of the album being something else. It was a feeling that I had that we needed to almost make a statement to say that we were moving beyond our roots into the bigger, wider world.

A lot of the books I was reading at the time were about the Weimar Era in Germany when there was a combination of incredible decadence and political unrest. I was looking at art by the wonderful George Grosz and Otto Dix. I was reading poetry by Bertolt Brecht and reading his plays. I always had a Brecht obsession. He was right at the heart of what was happening at that time. He was the political rock at the heart of that era which was surrounded by a decadence captured so wonderfully by Christopher Isherwood who would be a tremendous influence on David Bowie.

And Bowie's influence on *Days in Europa* shouldn't be discarded because this was at the time when Bowie had been living in Berlin and released Low. Low is my favourite album of all time. That's the Bowie album I listen to still. It's an album that influenced me greatly. It's full of despair. It combines the horror and terror of what Berlin was like during that period. It also captures the mystery of that incredible city which I still love. Berlin is my favourite city in the world and my favourite album in the world was made there by David Bowie, so the influences of those two things were pretty strong on *Days in Europa*.

By the time we had finished rehearsing, the decision was made that we would take all these new ideas that were inspired by all these different components into an environment that we had never been in before. Normally we just went into a studio and got on with it very quickly. But the idea this time was to make Stuart feel as comfortable as possible so that he wouldn't throw a wobbly again and walk out on the band.

We decided to work at Rockfield Studios in Wales just outside Monmouth. It was a residential studio. The live- in situation worked and we just concentrated on the work. For Stuart he was going to be working with his great hero, Bill Nelson. He was going to be in a very safe environment where he could have an almost normal existence where you have your own room. He could also of course have Sandra there, who would make him feel more at ease with everything. That was the plan, and we all felt confident that it would work.

Into The Valley

CHAPTER TWENTY-ONE

He arrived at Rockfield Studios to prepare work on *Days in Europa* full of optimism.

We'd, had a couple of hit singles with 'Into the Valley' and 'Masquerade'. Our new working relationship with Bill Nelson looked really positive and forward thinking and Rusty Egan had brought the sound of the rhythm section into the modern world. He had really encouraged us to try a different dynamic with some of our songs, to make them feel as if you could dance to them. So it was really an exciting moment to be at Rockfield where we would be living out of each other's pockets for the next couple of months.

It was a very isolated rural area outside of Monmouth but I think that suited what we intended to do. We were there to work and push The Skids' sound into a new area so we didn't want the distraction of being at home where we would obviously be carrying on with our domestic life. Well, apart from me of course because I didn't really have a home. And we didn't want to be in London because there was just too many distractions there so it was a really solid, strong idea to lock ourselves away to create a new sound and keep the whole thing as a private exercise and enterprise.

Bill Nelson had very clear ideas about our working methods. He wanted the band to play together in the studio, but really he just wanted each instrument caught independently so it was nice and clean. It was a new way of working because we always liked to play as a band and then get a great sense of how the song worked on tape and then start doing the overdubs. This was a different way of working, it was much cleaner, but it took longer and was boring for me as the singer.

Bill and Rusty Egan clashed from the first minute. Bill was a very sensitive, smart, intellectual guy and he just found Rusty's behaviour, his loud mouth and his opinions about everything, to be pretty vulgar. So they fought from the beginning, which was not a great start to the project. The rest of us started to fall in behind Bill and wished that Rusty would just get on with the job he was being paid to do and stop having an opinion about everything. About the guitar lines, about the keyboards, about the baseline — even about my melodies for the vocals. He was all over the project as if he was producing it. So we decided to get the majority of the drum tracks done as quickly as possible, then release Rusty back to London so he could get on with the other things in his life.

He invited some of his friends down whilst we were recording including Steve Strange who came because he was actually from the nearby town of Newport. I think he'd come down to see his mother then he came and hung out with us. I don't think he liked our music very much, it was still a bit too rough and punky for him, but we weren't so sure about him either. Although I must say, in all my dealings with Steve through the years, we always got on pretty fine and he was always very nice to me.

So we managed to get the majority of the drum tracks done within the first couple of weeks. The pressure gauge of Rusty disappearing off to London was truly fantastic because I think for the first time during the recording process for *Days in Europa* we could all relax. Stuart had disappeared for a little period when we were doing the drums, not because of his usual sense of disappointment with the rock and roll industry, just because he wanted to go home and see Sandra who was then going to come down and stay with him during recording, which was fine by the rest of us.

There was definitely a sense that the songs we were recording were very different from what we had done before. The rhythm, the pace, the emptiness within them was brand new to us. Normally we tried to fill everything up and give them an edge, an identity very quickly. But the identity of the songs were coming together in a studio for the first time, which was a new process for us. We were still very young at the time and not that sophisticated or experienced about what could and couldn't be done in a studio.

I never really enjoyed being in studios and for the most part I didn't really enjoy the slowness of the pace of *Days in Europa*. Our working day would start around 10:00 in the morning and then by 6:00 after we'd had dinner it was pretty clear that not much more work was going to be done. Maybe an occasional overdub here and there, but nothing particularly dramatic. When it got to the dinner hour Bill Nelson liked to have a glass of wine and just relax, so his pace of working was not what we were accustomed to, it was much slower than we would've liked. But at the same time it gave us plenty of time to be more analytical about what we were doing and how we were doing it.

In the evening, whilst we were waiting to eat, we would always play music that had affected us in some way. Bill had just got a hold of *Unknown Pleasures* by Joy Division and that really was the album that was the most prevalent sound during the recording of *Days in Europa*. Along with *Low* by David Bowie and the ambient records by Brian Eno.

It seemed to be the major diet of stuff we listened to. We also listened to some of Bill Nelson's new songs that he had created with Red Noise, which we liked very much. We were big fans of Red Noise and especially a track called 'Furniture Music', which was one of his key tracks from that project.

The lyrical content of our songs was pretty much defined by the time I reached the studio, but I started to do some more experimental things. For example when we had finished recording 'Animation', Bill reversed the track and I read a piece of spoken word poetry over the top of it called *Peaceful Times*. Just as a bit of fun late one evening when we were more relaxed, during the post-dinner period when not much work would be done, but we would try some mad stuff.

Peaceful Times came out of that experience and actually really worked, it had this strange, hypnotic, crazy feel about it. The words I wrote were again a reflection of this outward-looking young guy looking towards Europe rather than the USA. Most bands who were our contemporaries only ever thought about getting to America, I never really thought about America ever when I was in The Skids. It was more of a European connection and it's that connection with Europe that I feel to this day. So the poetry of *Peaceful Times,* the lyrics of 'The Olympian' and of course songs like 'Animation' really reflect a lot of my outward-looking views of being connected to the old world of Europe rather than the new world.

'Working for the Yankee Dollar' was a statement, a critique of the USA, American intervention and wars and America as an imperial force. It's a song we still play to this day and because of what's been happening in American politics recently it actually has more meaning today than it possibly had back then. So the atmosphere during the recording of *Days in Europa* was really good. It was fun, the band was getting on really well, especially after Rusty went back to London and Bill, myself and Stuart really connected.

We had a lot of laughs, Sandra was around and Stuart seemed much happier than he had been during the recording of *Scared to Dance*. So there was no essential dramas or sense that anything was going wrong. It was during this period that I started to think about the sleeve design.

The designing of sleeves had fallen into my lap from quite an early stage apart from the mishap for the *Wide Open* EP, which was done by Virgin, which we all hated, and then the simplicity of the 'Into the Valley' sleeve. Most of the sleeves, especially *Scared to Dance*, had been pretty cool. I wanted to take that a stage further now that it was thoroughly in my corner to work with. Stuart felt I had more of an eye and was more focused on the art world than he was, so it felt absolutely okay to allow me to get on with it.

With my interest in the Weimar period in Germany, that became a reflection of what I was thinking about and what might work for the sleeve. With the original album title planned as *The Olympian*, I found a poster from the infamous '36 Olympics in Berlin that felt absolutely perfect. The sleeve is done with a modicum of irony, but I had no idea that it was going to cause such a fuss when the album was released. People completely misunderstood the reason we used that sleeve and there's one thing for sure that The Skids never had any fascist bent whatsoever, we were always diehard socialists.

Politics were ingrained from our left-leaning, traditional Scottish working class background and we were absolutely appalled by anything to do with extreme right-wing ideology. So fascism and the fetish a lot of bands had for the Nazi party was certainly not part of our life and it's been something that's bugged me since making *Days in Europa* — the way some people misinterpreted that sleeve. It also associated me with some really dodgy politics, which has never been the case and I'm completely the opposite and absolutely abhor and loathe any form of fascism.

The sleeve was created through my guidance and it just looked magic to me, the way that the image worked with the context of the songs and the influence of the songs from a very specific period in history. I had no idea that people would look upon it as an image that celebrated some kind of fascism when actually it was a critique of the very same thing. I was advancing as a person at this time, I was still young and naïve, I was still fairly isolated in my own sense of personal values and self-worth. I had no particular relationship with anybody to speak of and was still having problems with my health on a pretty regular basis.

So none of that had gone away, it was always still there, it's just that I made it incredibly private and didn't really share it with any of the other band members. Bill Nelson was aware of it, as was Stuart obviously, and Bill was always very sympathetic during recording of *Days in Europa* when I had to disappear off into a dark room and sometimes spend twenty-four hours in there just until I felt better. But the general feeling in the studio was pretty good and all the influences of the books I was reading and the images that I liked by the artists I liked were being transformed into material for the album.

Especially artists like Georg Grosz, John Heartfield and Otto Dix who were definitely in the songs somewhere. Maybe not so obviously, but they were definitely in there. I felt that even though I was self- taught in all of these areas, that I was advancing, I was becoming more knowledgeable about a period that I was very interested in. More knowledgeable about creating and shaping words and more informed about how history works and how to make it work in a song. So this was really a magical moment to be with someone like Bill Nelson because he was also a self-taught person, but he had this real thirst for knowledge and he had much more experience than I did and was happy to share information.

He started to point me in the right direction with music, for example where Brian Eno's ambient music came from — born from the work of Erik Satie and suddenly I was listening to *Gymnopédies* or Gnossiennes, the wonderful piano pieces by Satie. I was listening to music that I'd never even considered listening to before, like the German band Can. Suddenly I could see the fantastic influence of that music on what was happening as punk was falling into the shadows and this new thing was emerging.

The thing that emerged of course which suffocated all of this, was something called 'new Romantics' which was just rubbish, stupid and idiotic. But at the same time it was a catalyst for using new sounds and new music and looking to Europe rather than America for influence. That certainly made a mark with me and the overall experience of recording *Days in Europa* was truly magical — I loved every minute of it. With the mixes that Bill Nelson did, I felt that we had moved on, they felt really strong and ambitious.

Alas our record company didn't feel the same way, Virgin Records were looking for a barrage of hits to follow up 'Into the Valley' and 'Masquerade'. They felt they were in the album like 'Charade' and 'Working for the Yankee Dollar', even 'Animation'. But they also felt that Bill Nelson's production had flattened The Skids' sound, he had taken the dynamic out of it and they were really, truly disappointed by the mixes he offered. So they called us in to have a powwow about the album and said, "listen, we're not happy with this."

We fought tooth and nail, Stuart and I, to defend the album and we wanted to release it as it was. The compromise we reached with Virgin is that they would allow someone called Mick Glossop to remix *Days in Europa* and that there would be two mixes available. Now this is where one of the great myths around The Skids can at last be resolved. There's a general feeling that the first release which had the yellow Olympian sleeve was banned. And that we were forced to change the sleeve and release the album in a different way, which is complete and utter bollocks.

The reality is that we released the yellow album, which was Bill Nelson's production. Then we made available a second album, which was remixed by Mick Glossop and it was put in a different sleeve so any Skids fan could make their own determination about which one they prefer because they did sound very different. One was the more experimental sound from Bill Nelson whereas Mick Glossop really understood the dynamic of The Skids, so he actually turned up the heat a little bit on some of the tracks that Bill had quite intentionally turned down.

You could hear the growl of the old Skids in those songs after Mick Glossop remixed it. So people ask me which my preferences are, I like both of them. I like the original one by Bill, I understand it does feel slightly flat in places and Mick Glossop really gave the album a kick up the arse and highlighted the dynamic elements of Stuart's guitar playing especially. He caught a very different mood from the album, so it was quite appropriate in my opinion that we used two different sleeves for what were two different albums.

Those two albums are still available to this day, so nothing was banned, there was no shock-horror, other than from a journalists' view. The same journalists I might add who never, ever criticised Joy Division who had, if you put that in a historical context, a pretty inappropriate name. Which changed and evolved into a New Order, which is pretty much just as bad. So never a word of criticism there, but we use an image and they come after us like we'd, done some terrible crime. Which we hadn't and I'm very proud of that sleeve to this day and very happy in this book to defend it.

Into The Valley

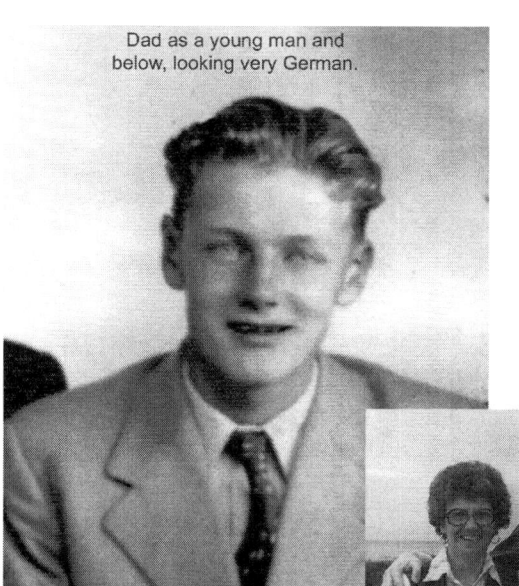
Dad as a young man and below, looking very German.

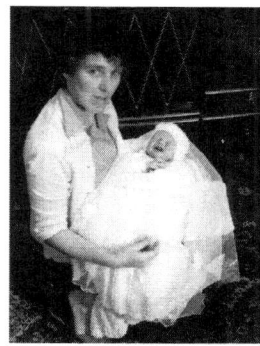
Mother with me as a baby.

My mother (left) with her sisters and Celtic captain Billy McNeil.

My younger brother Michael with Celtic captain and legend Billy McNeil.

With my brothers. John at the front and Brian and Michael behind him.
Francis was sadly dead when this was taken.

My brother Francis.

My mother with my daughter Edie.

Mother with my son Archie.

My father with Edie.

Belville, 1977.

Our first appearance at the Sheriff Court.

● The Skids, who this Friday release their debut single "Sweet Suburbia" pressed on white vinyl, are support on The Stranglers' forthcoming UK tour. Meanwhile the Scots group appear at London Music Machine tonight, Nashville (6) and Covent Garden Rock Garden (9).

Skids debut album

SCOTTISH Band the Skids are to release their debut album next month . . . followed by an extensive British tour in March.

'Scared To Dance' is released on February 22, preceded by the single taken from it — 'Into The Valley' — on February 9. On the live front the Skids play one "warm up" concert at the London Marquee on February 8 before beginning their tour at Newport Stowaway Club on February 28.

Other dates follow at: Cardiff Glamis Club March 1, Bristol University 2, York Pop Club 7, Leeds Fan Club 8, Birmingham Barbarellas 9, Plymouth Polytechnic 10, Stafford North Staffs Poly 14, Sheffield Limit Club 15, Hull College of Technology 16, Liverpool Erics (2 shows) 17, Edinburgh Tiffanys (2 shows) 19, Aberdeen City Hall 21.

More dates are likely to be added in the near future.

Dressing Room fun after a gig.

Hope & Anchor

Virgin Records promo shoot 1979 (*Mike Laye*)

Skids in action

THE SKIDS (above) have lined up a string of British gigs next month following the release of their new single, "A Woman In Winter", which comes out on November 28 on Virgin.

It's believed to be the first single to include a comic book story, drawn by Jill Mumford. The B-side of the single is a live version of "Working For The Yankee Dollar" recorded at their recent Hammersmith Odeon concert.

The group complete a European tour with The Jam next week and begin their British dates at Leicester University on November 29, continuing at Sheffield Polytechnic 30, Stirling University, December 1, Ayr Pavilion 2 and Dundee University 3 before nipping across to New York for their first American appearance at Hurrah's Club.

They return for more British dates at Bristol Colston Hall December 8, Exeter University 9, Hanley Victoria Hall 11, Leeds Polytechnic 13, Oxford New Theatre 14, Hull City Hall 15.

New-look Skids out on tour

THE SKIDS, whose line-up changes were announced in last week's paper, have now confirmed the dates for their British college tour next month.

The band, now made up of Richard Jobson and Stuart Adamson with ex-Zones bassist Russell Webb and drummer Mike Bailey, kick off at Manchester Polytechnic of March 6 and continue at Birmingham University 7, Colchester Essex University 8, Norwich East Anglian University 9, York University 10, Sheffield University 11, Bradford University 12, Hull University 13, Newcastle Polytechnic 14, Leicester Polytechnic 15, Swansea University College 17, Reading University 18, Nottingham Trent Olytechnic 19, Belfast Ulster Hall 21, Dublin Olympic Hall 22.

Jobson appears in Dunfermline district court this week with two friends charged with a breach of the peace.

Def changes

DEF LEPPARD have added gigs at Rickmansworth Town Hall February 25 and Bournemouth Town Hall 26 to their current tour and have replaced their Swansea gig on the 12th to Cheltenham Town Hall.

Top Of The Pops

Top Of The Pops

Skids

Performing 'Circus Games' on Top Of The Pops, 1980.

Berlin 1980
(*Paul Slattery*).

1980
(Virginia Turbett)

Virgin Records promo shoot 1980 (*Allan Ballard*)

July 1980 (*LFI*)

Hammersmith Odeon
(*Virginia Turbett*)

New York 1981
(*Virginia Turbett*)

Skids For Kids Tour 1981 (*Joe Stevens*)

Skids for the kids

THE SKIDS are lining up a series of school gigs to precede their British tour next month. The band are currently negotiating with Education Authorities in Liverpool, Manchester, Glasgow, Edinburgh and Dublin for the band to play lunchtime concerts in school playgrounds from the back of a lorry.

The first to be confirmed is at Ealing Fielding Middle School on September 19 at noon. This group will play for half an hour before making a personal appearance at Ealing Beggars Banquet records in the afternoon.

The Skids have previously played several matinee performances for school kids who can't attend normal concerts and say that these latest "Skids For Kids" dates are an extension of the desire to "bring rock and roll into the classroom or playground".

Kids' stuff

THE SKIDS' first 'Skids For Kids' playground appearance at Ealing's Fielding Middle School last Friday was cancelled by the headmaster after publicity for it meant that kids from other schools in the area took time off to become temporary pupils at the school.

The other dates are therefore not being publicly announced, although they will be taking place at Sheffield, Brighton, Glasgow, Edinburgh, Dunstable and Doncaster during The Skids' British tour.

Rehearsals

Above: The Skids 2017 back where it all started in Dunfermline for this publicity shot.
Below: Richard performing with the reformed band in 2017.
(*Gordon Smith*)

CHAPTER TWENTY-TWO

He prepared for the *Days in Europa* tour by setting up in the Glen Pavilion. I had this incredible ambition to make the Skids a very visual band that used a lot of the ideas that were inherently part of the lyrics of the songs, as part of our visual representation on stage. We organised to have an amazing backdrop, a big circular screen, which I think was borrowed from Pink Floyd, and on that we had projected a whole array of images from distant wars and conflicts, to fairly melancholy isolated stills, to shots of great triumph. The montage of images that were used came from many different quarters, chosen mostly by myself and edited together to present a new confident band.

We had completely absorbed ourselves in the preparation and the recording of *Days in Europa*, we wanted to do something special, and now was the time to get out there and play the whole thing. We had this crazy idea that we could play the whole album, which most people would never dream of doing because the audience weren't particularly familiar with the new songs. A lot of people would want to hear the obvious hits from *Scared to Dance* and the material we had released previously: 'Charles', 'Sweet Suburbia', 'The Saints are Coming', of course 'Into the Valley' and 'Masquerade'.

But we made the bold decision to say, no, we're not

going to do that, we're actually going to play the whole of *Days in Europa* from start to finish. We would come on stage to the backwards version of 'Animation', where I'm reading the poetry of *Peaceful Times*, and then go straight into 'Animation', the first track on the album, and go through all of the songs, and then come back on stage afterwards and play some of the more obvious Skids songs.

Our presentation of the new material was incredibly brave and ambitious. We also felt because there was so much keyboards involved that we would need to recruit a keyboard player. In a lot of people's eyes the Skids were essentially a guitar band based around the sound of Stuart Adamson, and having keyboards was anathema to what we were all about. We disagreed with that because we felt, having had this incredible experience working with Bill Nelson, we had pushed our sound as far as we could at that moment in time and we really needed to find that element that was essentially part of the album for the live performance.

We recruited a guy called Alastair Moore, who was known to both Stuart and Bill Simpson. He was a local guy who was classically trained, and we enrolled him for the tour. Aly was a complex character and had a great sense of humour. He was probably the least stylish person I've ever met in my life and wasn't best suited to the rock 'n' roll lifestyle, as he was born out of a completely different discipline, but nonetheless he understood what was needed and he was a great player. We decided to give it a go with him and see if he could make *Days in Europa*, come to fruition live.

The tour kicked off with a major gig at the Edinburgh Odeon, which has always been one of my favourite venues. It no longer exists, sadly, as a rock 'n' roll venue, but it was a large cinema that was often used for the opening and closing of the Edinburgh film festival and had recently been developed into a venue for bands to play. It was a really wide venue that held a lot of people and had a magical sound. This is where we unleashed *Days in Europa* for the first time, and it was a tremendously exciting moment for me because it was an album that I was so immersed in. I think I had more to do with *Days in Europa* than I had, had with *Scared to Dance*.

I felt that the visual ideas were really mine to push through. I wanted it all to work really well. I didn't want us to end up with egg on our face and be accused of being pretentious. We presented that show that evening in Edinburgh, and it was truly one of the great Skids gigs. The response we got was amazing and it gave us the idea that we could go on tour and just play the whole album and be brave and proud.

We were even joined on stage during the gig by Bill Nelson, and we did a version of the classic Be-Bop Deluxe song, 'Panic in the World'. It felt right, everything felt right. We embarked on a long tour. Rusty still played drums and he was actually pretty amazing on the tour. He gave us a thundering dynamic that we'd never had before with Tom. He also gave us a bit of class in the elegance of his drumming. It was great to have him on the stage, but God, he was a nightmare to deal with on a daily basis, because he was always telling us what we should be wearing, what we should be saying, how we should be behaving.

I remember we were on *Top of the Pops* with him, I think with 'Working for the Yankee Dollar', and he told me afterwards that his friend said there was only one person in the band that was worth looking at and that was him. That pretty much summed up Rusty, although underneath all that bullshit, he actually is a pretty decent guy and I remain friendly with him to this day, although he's still exactly the same: you have a conversation with him, it's only going to be going one way, and that is you're going to be listening to him talking about himself.

But we embarked on the tour with a sense of great optimism and a feeling that we had moved on as a band. We were very brave doing the whole album, but we realised after about three days the amazing, exciting performance at the Edinburgh Odeon would not be replicated around the country, because people wanted to hear 'Into the Valley', and they were screaming for that idiotic, stupid song of ours, 'TV Stars', with a chorus of "Albert Tatlock", whilst we were standing there trying to do something quite serious and it became quite disappointing.

Stuart and I talked about it three or four days into the tour and said, we're going to have to change this, we're going to have to actually put the other songs into the set, because otherwise we're doing nothing but disappointing people. We eventually compromised and changed the set on the tour and involved more of the other songs. The idea that we would just play the whole album day after day pretty much evaporated after a week when it just wasn't working. Especially in England, it just didn't work. We had to put the other songs in there, although it was sad that, that happened.

We were always aware that the audience were the most important part of our live show. If they weren't happy, then we hadn't delivered. Of course it was good to challenge them, but at the same time, people had paid hard-earned cash to come and see us, and the Skids had essentially a working-class following. Money would have not been easy to find to come and see us. The idea that they would have left the gig unhappy and slightly frustrated was a red light to us. We quite rightly were grown up about it and made the decision that we would involve the other songs.

The tour carried on and in some ways it had started off so incredibly well with an amazing high, but overall I didn't really enjoy that tour so much. Something felt wrong about it and I got a sense again of Stuart going back into his normal ways of being deeply unhappy and frustrated with having to be on tour and be part of the rock 'n' roll industry when he just wanted to be back in Dunfermline with Sandra. He had put a deposit down on a flat, something we thought that old people did, not young people like us, and it seemed more and more that he was focussed on having a normal life outside of the band, whereas of course I was doing the opposite.

I was hanging out with Rusty and Steve Strange in London and having a pretty crazy time. The interaction between Stuart and I seemed to be falling by the wayside as he spent more and more time with Sandra. When we reached the end of the tour, we felt that the keyboards weren't really working and Ali, although he was a nice guy, didn't really fit into the band. The decision was made that we would continue without him. I can't quite recall now how that decision was reached although I am absolutely certain that it was Stuart's because all musical decisions were made by him.

Unfortunately he didn't tell Bill who was deeply offended by the fact that he hadn't been told and was also very, very angry about it. Post the tour, we'd been a regular again on *Top of the Pops* with 'Working for the Yankee Dollar' and previous to that 'Charade'. It suddenly was brought to my attention that Bill didn't want anything to do with the band anymore. He felt he had been humiliated by not being involved in the decision with his friend Alistair and also because he wasn't really involved in the actual writing process.

Any money that was being made from publishing he

wasn't part of, so he felt he'd just been excluded from the whole thing. He threw his toys out of the pram and walked off, which was quite a shock at the time. Bill leaving was more of a shock than Tom, because Bill was one of the founder members, he was very consistent as a personality, unlike Stuart who was very inconsistent, and of course I was pretty crazy. In retrospect, my being in London and hanging out with all different kinds of people and bringing those experiences back, rather than bringing myself closer to the band was actually pushing me further away without me even realising.

I was still only 18 years old and just grabbing each day by the horns and shaking it, and that was for a variety of reasons. My expectations of hanging around, as in living for a longer period, were pretty much nil. My action was to enjoy every day as much as I possibly could, whereas I think Bill saw it as more of a career. He was dismayed by the direction it was going and also big decisions being made without him ever being brought into the actual discussion.

I also think something very odd was happening. We were on these TV programmes. Our performances, which you can still see on YouTube, were pretty idiotic. I'm dressed like a fool and starting to behave like a fool. I don't know if I was losing my mind at the time, maybe it was just the sheer excitement of the social life that I was having, which was tremendously life affirming in some ways. Sometimes I'd come back to rehearse and we'd be back to our little space in the garage, and it was almost like a house of cards had fallen down. It just seemed so small and inconsequential and provincial that it just felt like the band weren't moving on after all these attempts through *Days in Europa* to create a new identity and a new sound and a new vision.

Actually, the underlying aspects of the band were still the

same. The management had no vision for us, there was no sense of where this could really go, and I think at that point in time, we really need to change things. It was then that I took Bill Nelson's advice and brought in his management company Arnakata, which would in fact prove to be a disastrous decision.

Into The Valley

CHAPTER TWENTY-THREE

After the strange *Days in Europa* tour there was feeling that this great adventure we had been on in was pushing our punk origins into a new sound. By looking further afield from where the band had started out from, not just geographically in Scotland, but also culturally; Evolving into a more sophisticated group, but keeping all of the ingredients that made the Skids exciting in the first place. Those ingredients were obviously Stuart's very unique guitar style that had an edge, lyrics that in some way related to the world around us and the songs having a passion and ferociousness about them.

The fallout from the flatness of Bill Nelson's production caused a little bit of disarray within the band in the sense that we truly believed in Bill, but we had allowed the record company to determine that the sound just didn't have the edge that it needed. Therefore bringing in Mick Glossop to remix the album was almost essential to get back to what we were all about. I think we knew that there was something missing in that album, but at the same time we were so proud of those new songs and the fact that we had been brave enough to try something new.

So the compromise didn't make us feel too bad and also we had been strong with the record company to say that we wanted the original recording to exist. Bill Nelson was aware of all of this and he was aware that it was a record company decision not ours. He was also aware that we fought very hard to retain the integrity of the first version of the album and its production values. So it never affected our friendship in any way, in fact my personal friendship with Bill Nelson after working on *Days in Europa* really grew.

I started to spend a bit of time at his house in Yorkshire and listening to music with him. He would point me in the direction of some books that he was interested in — Jean Cocteau and the world around Cocteau. Which was a world of movies, art and fashion and he was one of the great French stylists of the period before World War Two. Some of his movies, which Bill introduced me to, were pretty incredible, *Beauty and the Beast, The Blood of a Poet*. These were just amazing cinematic hyper stylised works that made an indelible print on the way I thought at the time.

So along with Bill I became a Cocteau aficionado. Bill had started his own label called Cocteau Records and he knew that I had been adapting work by a French writer, Marguerite Duras, who I had been introduced to by some of my French friends in Belgium.

He asked me if I might be interested in doing a spoken word record for Cocteau Records. I had been working with a girl called Virginia Astley and some of her friends, doing very small, unique performances at a club organised by Richard Strange. Richard started this Dada-esque cabaret club, Cabaret Futura, in the heart of London's West End and invited a whole array of different types of performers.

It would go on to become quite a famous club in London at the time, around the Leicester Square area in the old Latin Quarter. So there was me doing my spoken word adaptations of Marguerite Duras or Sylvia Plath's Daddy and some other poems that I'd written, occasionally with a musical accompaniment by Virginia. Or I'd be joined sometimes by the Frank Chickens, the Japanese performers or the actor Keith Allen. I remember doing the very first one where he used a steak pie as a glove puppet, which was very, very funny.

Cabaret Futura had a lot of different qualities and I really enjoyed the madness of it. Again, it made me feel like I was inhabiting a world in a city that was part of Europe. So it felt like it was connected in some ways to the crazy world of Berlin in the 1920s and '30s before the Nazis took power and it also felt like some of the more radical clubs in Paris during the same period.

Its essential influences were definitely from them, but the acts that were performing in Cabaret Futura were bringing something a little bit more contemporary to the table. I started to do more work with Virginia and a few other people to create music that I would use as the layer and then read on top. The music was a combination of work by Eric Satie or original pieces composed by Virginia and her friends.

I took the idea to Virgin, who were thought it was ridiculous, that it was pompous and frustrating, and that I should be thinking about the next Skids album at this point in time. My explanation to them was I just needed a little break. The *Days in Europa* tour had been exhausting, the problem that it caused we hadn't yet solved because we needed to find a new bass player. I just wanted to do something for myself and if it wasn't any good then they could say don't release it, but if it was going to be on Cocteau Records probably nobody would even notice it was being released anyway.

I managed to convince them to let me get on with it. They allowed me to go and record in the barge, which is one of those small recording studios in an area around near Maida Vale on one of the canals in Little Venice. It was a really amazing environment that I really liked. The Skids had already done some demos there. I think it was again the romanticism and peculiarity of recording in such a strange environment which appealed to me.

I always really hated, and still to this day hate, a studio environment that's just so clinical. It has no atmosphere and no history. They're just modern boxes where people work and I really hated that, it bored me senseless. So the idea behind the barge was really exciting and we only had one day to record all of these pieces of spoken word and music. But we managed to do it, I got lots of help from my new bunch of close friends. John McGeoch, helped out and Virginia was very, very helpful.

At that point in time I met a guy called Russell Webb, who also helped a little bit with some of the performances I was doing at Cabaret Futura. Russell had been in a band from Glasgow called the Zones who we knew and respected. They had been signed to Arista Records but it just hadn't happened for them. Russell was a great bass player, a very good musician and the Zones were splitting up. So it looked like we may have found a good fit for The Skids.

He was a very, very accomplished player and I got on with him at that point in time, so I felt it might be good for Stuart to have a stronger musical companion working with him and take some of the pressure off because Russell also had ambitions to get involved with writing. So all of these things were happening at a similar time, it was almost like every day brought along another adventure.

It was at that time, before we decided to start working as The Skids again and offer Russell Webb the position as the bass player, that I decided to go off on a little tour of Europe.

I performed one evening with Bill Nelson in Brussels

at the Plan K, which had been arranged by a girl I'd met in London called Annik, she worked at the Belgian Embassy as one of the cultural attaches. She was also the girlfriend of Ian Curtis and she was a really brilliant person, who has sadly passed away now. She was really very supportive of what I was trying to do and we got on extraordinarily well. I met her with Ian who I'd met before when I had sung for the Stranglers when Hugh Cornwell had been put in prison for possession of drugs. Along with other guests I sang one evening with the Stranglers at London's Rainbow Theatre in April 1980. Ian Curtis was a part of Joy Division that was the support act on that particular night.

Ian had a massive epileptic seizure on stage. After the show when he was feeling better, I talked to him, obviously we had the same condition and shared some of our common anxieties. I met him again with Annik at an Iggy Pop gig in the Music Machine in Camden and we hung out and really got on very, very well. We felt we had a special bond because we had a condition that affected both of us, in different ways of course. But still it was a very private condition in some ways... for me at least. His condition had become more public because he was having seizures during his live performances that was affecting his mental health I think.

Ian was a genuine guy and I really liked talking to him about everything from music to art. Annik encouraged me to come out and perform in Brussels at the Plan K where I met a guy called Michel Duval who had heard the Cocteau Records release of my poetry and asked if I'll be interested in doing some work with his new company, Crépuscule, which had a relationship with Factory Records in England, which of course was the home of Joy Division.

This was really exciting. So suddenly I was in a Brussels studio and I was recording a whole second spoken work

Into The Valley

album for Crépuscule and loved every minute of it working with a variety of different musicians. The studio was really super cool and I went in and wrote some crazy poetry. One of them was called *Armoury Show*, which of course I would use later as the name of the band I would create after The Skids. I really enjoyed the freedom of just going into a studio and expressing myself through the spoken word.

I had some beautiful piano music that was being played by Michel's girlfriend's sister Cecile and lots of Satie music. Then I started to play a very particular ambient type of piano. Michel wanted to do an album of an imaginary journey through Europe and North Africa and beyond, all the way to Japan which he encouraged me to create. These things were not done in months but immediately. It was still that crazy punk ethos of, I'm just going to do this. I'm going to make this happen and let's do it today, why not?

I used the Brussels base as a way of suddenly pushing myself further into Europe, so I travelled by train from Brussels to Amsterdam and hung out with new friends I'd made there. Then from Amsterdam took the train to Hamburg and went to see the wonderful St. Pauli, who were my football team, who I still support to this day. I love the whole ethos of St. Pauli.

I've been a fan of the team from way back in the late '70s and early '80s. They were like a punk football team, based in the district of St. Pauli in Hamburg, which was where all the punk squatters lived. So it made sense that they had a punk following, which was really magical. From there I took the train to Berlin and Berlin became the city that I really fell in love with. I had a girlfriend there briefly called Caroline who was really very special, but she wasn't very well. For a variety of reasons, she suffered from terrible depression and unfortunately committed suicide in the apartment we briefly shared in Kreuzberg.

I saw a photograph the other day of me standing by the Berlin Wall looking glum. It was the week after her death. I've never been an emotional person. Never able to shed tears. Thats not something to be proud of. I had a person that at last I shared something with, books, music, maybe even love. Then she was gone. It was that quick. When I have quiet moments to myself I find myself thinking about her a lot. Because of the Internet, photographs keep surfacing of that period in Berlin, which of course brings it all back. So many people died young during that era, either through drugs or depression and suicide. It hurts.

It was a very dramatic time where all of these things just seemed to happen at the same time. So after Caroline's death I was in no doubt I needed to return to The Skids and just get on with something else, something that wasn't just me on my own and something that had a ferocity about it. I needed to be busy, to not dwell on events. I think that really was the spark to get back to the UK and start thinking about what was to become *The Absolute Game*. The title of that album, based on what had just happened should tell you everything you need to know.

Into The Valley

CHAPTER TWENTY-FOUR

It felt strange being back in the UK after my journey into the European heartland, spending time in the great cities of Paris and Brussels, but mostly Berlin, which ended in tragedy. The feeling inside at that moment was that I just needed to do something with other people. A lot of the spoken-word poetry stuff I'd been doing with Crépuscule in Belgium was pretty much on my own. Occasionally I would bring in other musicians to work with, but it was not the same as a group environment, and I needed to be back in the situation where you could bounce ideas off other people and be inspired by the energy of songwriting.

I was living in Edith Grove in Chelsea at the bottom of the King's Road, as I had kept a room in a flat there, but I went straight to Scotland and hooked up with Stuart, who told me who was to become our new drummer — Mike Baillie. Mike had been a local guy who'd played in bands like Matt Vinyl and the Decorators. He was from Dunfermline and he had played on the last date of the *Days in Europa* tour up in Aberdeen. He was a great guy, I've always had a tremendous respect for Mike, and it was great to have him on board.

It felt like Stuart was getting motivated into reconfiguring the band and thinking about new songs. We started to play around with some exciting ideas. You could see the beginning of songs like 'Arena', 'Hurry On Boys' and 'A Woman in

Winter'. The genesis of these songs started to appear just between him and I as we started knocking them together. Also in Stuart's own personal life he took his romance with Sandra a stage further. They had decided to get married and he had a really positive energy going on around him.

He definitely felt that my absence and journey into Europe had left a bit of a gaping black hole between our friendship and songwriting relationship, but it seemed to me at least that getting back into working again happened very quickly. We started to bounce ideas off one another and I felt that these songs could actually be going somewhere. We needed to find a bass player and we felt that it could be Russell Webb, who was based in London, so we decided to try him out in a rehearsal space there.

We immediately got into work in this fairly cold, abandoned warehouse space in North London, and the songs started to come together very, very quickly. We demoed some of them with Mick Glossop, who was going to be our producer on this new project. It all seemed to work quite well in the early days.

Russell was a very accomplished musician, he had some ideas that were interesting, and although he seemed to have a negative view of Mike and Mike's drumming ability from a very early stage, we made it clear to him that we felt Mike was our guy and we wanted a sense of the band's identity to continue, which was still very Dunfermline and Scottish in its origins. The early period of working on *The Absolute Game* and preparing the songs that would eventually make it to the album was really not challenging at all. It was for me personally, a necessity to try and put behind me the various adventures in Europe that had left me feeling somewhat distraught.

When I got down to writing the lyrics for a lot of these

new songs, I suddenly connected them to really what was going on inside my head, because although I hid it from everybody, my health was not in a good place. I didn't feel strong, I felt very weak. My psychological state was pretty damaged from my European journey. I felt a little bit lost in the sense of the normal isolation I experienced, and that had been compounded with all those recent events.

I think for the first time the songs became really reflective of that mood. Whereas before the songs in their abstraction were about how I saw the world both historically and how it reflected on the modern day. The new songs seemed to be about my own, very fragile state of mind, although I don't think it was that obvious to the other members of the band.

If you start to look at songs like 'Goodbye Civilian', 'Hurry On Boys' and 'Circus Games', the lyrical content are definitely illustrations of, or little stories or narratives about, what I had been going through, and I was not in a good place.

I did feel vulnerable, if not occasionally suicidal, and I did feel, even though I was back in London, it wasn't exciting in the same way. The flat in the King's Road just felt cold and dangerous, I was in there on my own and it didn't feel good. This was a strange period that I was going through, and if you were to analyse the lyrics of any of these songs, particularly 'Goodbye Civilian', they are little reflections of the mood that I was in. A sense of despair really set in.

The events in Berlin were haunting me and my health was a mess. I had nobody to talk to and eventually started spending too much time my own. That was a disaster. People in that state of mind need to be with other human beings. Isolation is the beginning of the end. There were really scary days when, without over sentimentalising this story, I didn't want to continue. I felt there was nothing to continue for. Even though I was in a successful band and they had a decent fanbase who were anticipating the new music with great excitement. The loss of Bill Simpson hadn't caused too many tremors, and the recruitment of Mike Baillie was a really strong thing for us to have done. Plus Russell Webb became a musical force in the band, but normally when working with the Skids in the preparatory stages of the music and then going on to the recording, I always worked closely with Stuart. I had to deal with Stuart's moods and sense of dislocation from the music industry and his own despair about being in a band and wanting to go home and be with Sandra. Not this time.

During *The Absolute Game*, I didn't feel that anymore, I actually felt a little bit more selfish, I was more concerned about my own well-being and state of mind. We had taken on the new management company Arnakata, a guy called Mike Dolan, which was Bill Nelson's management company, and they were a pretty slick outfit. They had an array of different acts, from Judas Priest to Dollar, to obviously Bill Nelson and us, as well as The Tourists, who were soon to become The Eurythmics. They felt like a proper management agency, and we as a band felt at last we needed somebody to guide our fortunes in the right direction so it wasn't such a messy affair.

Traditionally the Skids management was just a mess. Behind the scenes, the management organisation was just pretty much disastrous. There was no plan; it was just reacting to whatever was put in front of it on a daily basis rather than actually having a forward-thinking plan. I think probably that's one of the reasons that Adamson felt so disturbed by the music industry, because our world didn't seem to have any structure, as such; therefore, you start to feel paranoid about the whole thing.

But even having Arnakata there, with their super slick, big, beautiful office in the Marble Arch area of London, didn't make me feel any better. I was in the strangest of strange places. I think I made the decision to use my mood and feeling in the songs. Certainly the mood of those songs when listening to them again now, is definitely a reflection of a very dangerous place that I found myself in. The only way out of this dangerous state of mind was to work and that's what I did. I got on with writing, making sure that I didn't spend too much time alone. I went to exhibitions, events where there were lots of people, even to football matches. But mostly I was busy writing lyrics during the preparation of the songs through rehearsal, before we went into a studio with Mick Glossop.

Mick was a really great guy and I really loved working with him. I found him a thoroughly decent man. He was an immensely talented guy who was both the engineer who controlled the desk and the guy in charge of the overall sound of where the Skids were going with *The Absolute Game*. We talked to him about how we wanted it to be a return to the high energy that could have been found in songs like 'Masquerade', 'The Saints Are Coming', 'Into the Valley', and also the way he remixed songs like 'Working for the Yankee Dollar', to give it that energy again that we felt maybe had been flattened a little.

The focus, essentially, was on Stuart's guitar playing and that was really good, because it got Stuart thinking about what he wanted from this album. It was important that the focus was put in that direction, and it seemed to alleviate some of his moods, but not all of them. Mike and Stuart were staying in a hotel in Notting Hill Gate for months as we prepared for the record. I wasn't and Stuart disappeared on many occasions back to Scotland, unannounced, and then would turn up two or three days later as if nothing had happened.

The one thing Stuart never did when he disappeared was he never told us he was going to disappear, he never told us when he was going to come back, and he never apologised once in the history of the band for doing that to us, but that was him. But besides all these kinds of almost perennial problems with him, the writing process had gone very well, and then the decision was made that we were going to once again go into a closed environment, because Virgin Records felt we worked better that way.

This time they wanted us to work in their studio so they could be closer to the album, not so far away like Rockfield in Wales. They had a studio in Oxfordshire called The Manor, where we had done bits and pieces before, and it was a really great place. Not too isolated, because the town of Oxford was only a few miles away, so it gave you something else to do on the days that you weren't working.

We agreed that it was a good idea to go there and it was a good idea to work with Mick Glossop, for sure, and although we were going to work as a four-piece band, we had agreed we would use keyboards on some of the tracks. But essentially the focus of the album was back to Stuart's guitar playing. That certainly was the blueprint for the record as we took off the rough edges of the songs in rehearsal and started to get ready to actually make the move to recording.

CHAPTER TWENTY-FIVE

Before we moved on to The Manor to start recording, I needed to find a new place to live.

The place in Chelsea was driving me crazy, and I was very fortunately offered a room in a mews house in Kensington by Lisa Anderson, who was the head of international marketing at Virgin and the wife of Bram Tchaikovsky, who had formerly been in The Motors. I think she realised that my health was not in the most wonderful situation and that maybe I needed a more solid base before we started to record our third album.

She was also aware, and this was something that people forgot, that I was still really very young, I was only 19 years old, and had been through quite a lot by this time. My worldly experiences were weighing down on me somewhat. I think she spotted that. It was really a nice place to live. She was a really lovely woman and cooked great food, although Lisa and Bram were away all the time so the house was mostly empty. As such I was able to spend time there, on my own and use it as a base to work harder, read and write more lyrics.

I certainly never used it as a party base, because that was so off the radar. I was locked in my own thoughts and in my own world and also preparing for this new album and trying to maintain a sense of enthusiasm that everybody else seemed to have through the rehearsal stage as we progressed towards the recording studio in Oxfordshire.

The relationship with Arnakarta was very strange. My immediate response was that they were going to open up all kinds of new avenues for us with their experience, but it just didn't seem to be working that way. I often queried how genuinely interested they were in the band. Were they more interested in getting a share of our publishing and taking a percentage of the new songs we were writing? Which seemed to be more of what they were about than actually motivating the band on to a higher level, which was very disappointing.

When we eventually arrived at The Manor I was feeling a little bit better about life just because I had a nicer place to live and felt a bit safer there. Under the guidance of Mick who cut a big brother/father figure throughout the next couple of months we worked on the album. He was a very solid guy who understood the tensions in a band and also understood that I was hanging on for dear life at this point in time.

There was a couple who looked after the food there, David and Valerie, who were really sweet, and I retained my friendship with them even to this day. They were great. It was David, actually, in many ways who started to say to me, maybe I should start to eat more regularly and eat better — these things might help, which in fact they did. The Manor was a beautiful, amazing place. It had a swimming pool, a lot of land, and inside we had our own bedrooms and our own space. We were looked after incredibly well, with breakfast, lunch, and dinner, and we could have anything we wanted at any point in time.

There was a large snooker table, a television room where we watched movies together as a band and had a lot of laughs, and we always had a game of snooker every evening after the recording session. We had decided that we would try and have regular working hours, which was unusual in a residential studio, but we thought, maybe let's try and do this from nine in the morning to maybe eight o'clock in the evening and then everybody can have a break.

That was a really solidly good idea, which came from Mick Glossop, a very organised man who understood that even though we had rehearsed all the songs and we were ready to play them that there was still a way to go to make these songs really work. But the one thing he understood was that the band wanted to record at a really quick pace. After the experience with Bill Nelson where everything was so slow, he totally got that.

Once Mike Baillie had got his confidence in place, he really went through the drums very, very quickly, which we got down first, and I actually think Mike's drumming on the album is absolutely exceptional. I think the performances from Mike and the guitar work from Stuart on *The Absolute Game* are tremendous. They're the highlights of the album without a doubt. It had an energy there because we were working quicker, it felt safe, and I started to feel just a little bit better about life. I was finalising a lot of the lyrics and trying to make the ones which were a bit more experimental, like 'Arena', come into the fold a little bit more. There was a good feeling during the start of the recording. Stuart had Sandra with him, he didn't feel so distant and isolated as he sometimes did, and other than Mike occasionally feeling bullied by Russell, the general feeling was pretty good. I think that's because Mick Glossop set it all up beforehand in such a way that we would go in there and we were ready, we weren't making it up on the day.

We were very organised. He made it very methodical

and when Stuart needed a break from the guitar playing, he would bring me in and we would try the vocals. He knew that with me you'd only ever get two or three chances and then if it didn't work, don't push it because it just wouldn't get any better, only worse. But because the atmosphere was good, the vocals came pretty quickly and started to have a really strong, embedded connection with the songs, which then inspired a lot of the overdubs to be done, which Stuart was the main player in, of course.

Because everything seemed to be in place, the songs had a power and an edge, and it was beginning to feel like we had created, or we were beginning to create at least, a really strong album. Maybe, possibly the strongest of all the Skids albums, because it seemed to have the power of *Scared to Dance* but the consistency of *Days in Europa*. I can't really remember much tension throughout the whole experience. The band weren't taking drugs or drinking. I think the guys probably had a beer now and again, but essentially there was nothing like that going on. We were taking the job very, very seriously.

I think that's what Mick wanted from us, he wanted us to feel that this was a game changer for the band, that it was time to step up to a bigger table, to start thinking beyond our strong fanbase, think about America, think about the rest of Europe, consider the band becoming a more powerful force. He was trying everything within his powers to push all the melodic elements of the Skids. He didn't try and bury the more experimental stuff, but he tried to make more sense of it, I think, whereas before we had been indulgent and were just allowed to get on with whatever we wanted.

Now the questions were being asked: why do you want to have that structure to the song or arrangement, why do you want to have those kinds of lyrics? At last, really, somebody was asking the proper questions, and if you didn't have the answer, then I think you had to give up. It was really important that we were all on the same page and understood why we were doing what we were doing and what it represented. There was no room for that self-indulgence. There was self-indulgence on my part, of course, because the lyrics of each song in many ways were connected to how I was feeling after my time in Europe and the ramifications of that.

The album kicks off with 'Circus Games', which was released as a single. It has an urgency and an energy, and the power comes straightaway from the sequencer, then into a classic Stuart Adamson guitar line. Lyrically it is about the corruption of innocence, which is pretty much the underlying theme of the album. For me personally, I felt the world had taken a very cynical turn, especially in my own private life. In some ways the song reflected that. It was my idea to use the kids singing in the chorus, and we used a lot of the people who worked at The Manor. We got their children in one weekend when they were not at school and recorded them.

It was great fun conducting them. They were super kids, and it gave the song another level. It wouldn't have had if it was just Stuart, myself and the rest of the band doing the backing vocals. Again the work by the guys, and especially Mick, to just give this song a force was exceptional. The last verse of the song is personally crushing. It's really a tough thing to listen to, and is very reflective of how my life was at the time and what had just happened. Even today playing the song live, it still has a real power for me.

The song that followed was an old Skids song wereinvented called 'Out of Town'. Again, a brilliant, classic Stuart Adamson guitar line, very melodic and powerful — all the elements that you would associate with early Skids, the oh-oh chanting, and a song that could be sung along with. It's again a very self-reflective song about addiction and suicide, and the chorus line of need to run, need to hide, that's just how I felt at that moment in time, and The Manor, where we were recording, was just the place to hide away for a while.

'Out of Town' is a ferocious Skids song and it's amazing to think I first wrote those words when I was 15, and Stuart put the music to it. It still works to this day, it's still got an incessant energy. 'Goodbye Civilian', which followed it, was I think where the Skids were trying to find that space between *Days in Europa* and the old Skids sound. It's got a little bit of that magical synthetic quality, but at the same time it's got a really beautiful guitar line. It was written as a farewell letter, which is a bit sentimental to say now, but it's a biographical song, of course.

It tries to depict the state of mind you're in after you've had an epileptic seizure and a feeling that life's not really worth living. I always think of it as my Berlin song, which may be a bit odd to people, but it always reminds me of the city. 'The Children Saw the Shame' followed that track, and again it's classic Adamson guitar. It almost sounds a little bit like Bill Nelson in places. The theme of innocence lost is recurring here again and with a really powerful chorus, it's got such a strong chorus line.

The album just comes hard at you, from 'Circus Games', 'Out of Town', 'Goodbye Civilian', 'The Children Saw the Shame', and then calms down with the very elegant, beautiful 'A Woman in Winter'. Again a song that became a film. I turned it into a movie, and the movie narrative takes the song in an even more personal direction. I'd been reading about the largest refugee crisis in world history after World War II. Germans from all parts of Eastern Europe all the way down to the Czech Republic were basically forced out of their homes violently after the war.

It created a refugee crisis of nearly twelve million people, of which many starved to death and were violently beaten. It's something that's not talked about because people often regard it as, well, that's what happens if you wage war, but it's one of the great crimes of the 20th century that nobody ever talks about. 'A Woman in Winter' and later on in the album 'The Devil's Decade' reflect the stuff that I was reading, which I hadn't known about. I don't think many people had at that time realised that there was such an incredible human tragedy and crime that had been committed.

One of the most haunting things when you hear 'A Woman in Winter' is Stuart's very sweet vocal when he's doing the oh-oh chant. He had a very sweet voice, but he does sound very ghostly, and the irony, of course, of all of this is that my feeling about my own personal well- being was not in a good place and I wasn't sure if I'd even make it through the recording.

You get to songs like 'One Decree', which sounds like a hymn, a desperate hymn of some kind asking for answers. Then to 'Arena', which is definitely the saddest song on the album. It truly captures where my head was, again with that beautiful guitar line followed by the chant at the end. It really reminds me of being in Berlin in 1979, and occasionally when I hear the song, it makes me want to weep. The irony, of course, is that I'm still here and Stuart Adamson's dead, and it was not me who committed suicide, it was Stuart, which is still something that shocks me to this day. I can't really make sense of that at all.

But certainly during the recording of *The Absolute Game*, there was no doubt in my mind that if you fall into these dark places and just keep on falling and falling that there's sometimes no way back. My way back was through the creative process of making an album that was substantial, that had a beauty and energy about it. That I think saved me; otherwise, if the album had been weak and the songs had been less than they should have been and we hadn't pushed ourselves to create something elegant but ferocious, then I'm absolutely certain I wouldn't have come through that period. It would have been a disaster for me.

We were well guided by Mick Glossop, who to this day remains a 100% solid human being, and a friend. And the band delivered, It was a new band after all, and we managed to create something quite magical. In many ways probably the most powerful Skids album of all of them. Sadly without realising, as we left the studio with a really strong album that our record company Virgin were really enthusiastic about, I had no idea that would be the last album I would ever make with Stuart Adamson, this would be the last time we would ever be together in a proper studio recording a Skids album.

CHAPTER TWENTY-SIX

We were looking at doing an extensive tour to promote *The Absolute Game* and it was going to be the largest tour we had ever undertaken. We were going to be playing some of the most iconic venues in the United Kingdom, including Hammersmith Odeon. So, we did feel that we were stepping up to another level in the domestic market. The decision was made to do a full-blown rehearsal, but instead of doing it as usual in Dunfermline, we decided to go back to Rockfield, where they had a rehearsal space and live-in accommodation just down the road from the main studio. We arrived there with a sense of fulfilment. That we had made *The Absolute Game* our successful album, according to our record company people, essentially they were right, it was incredibly strong.

The only downside of all of this is the management company decided that they no longer wanted to work with us and they gave no reason whatsoever why. I think they had their own business problems, and we were caught in the crossfire of that. They just said they didn't want to continue with us, which was a bit of a shock, although we had been pretty much disappointed with them anyway. I think Stuart found the main guy, to be quite sleazy and any social interaction we had with them was always in classic rock 'n' roll environments like Morton's in Barclay Square in Central London, the kind of place you might bump into Elton John's manager or Rod Stewart or someone of that ilk.

So they weren't really the right fit for us, although we thought at the time it might work, because they might take us to another level. But again, we had made another mistake in our desperation to get a stable organisation behind us, which, again, made everybody feel pretty insecure about where all this might be going. So the idea of going to Rockfield to rehearse was a good one and I think we all felt we needed to bond further with the old songs, because Russell and Mike hadn't really played songs from *Scared to Dance* and *Days in Europa* as yet. We needed to find a way to mix all the classic Skids songs together with the new songs and build a really strong set. The first couple of days there we did absolutely nothing. We actually bought fishing rods and went fishing by the river at the back of the rehearsal space. Simple Minds were recording in the main studio, so we got ourselves dressed up in crash helmets and balaclavas and raided Simple Minds in the middle of one of their recording sessions and absolutely terrorised them with our insanity.

Simple Minds were great guys and we always had, or

certainly I always had a very strong friendship with Jim Kerr and Charlie, Mick and Dan. We always got on really, really well. When I was living in mainland Europe I would often find myself jumping on the train and going down to see them in Paris or Amsterdam or wherever they were playing. We had played with them when they were Johnny and the Self-Abusers and came through to Dunfermline. They tried to steal all our equipment. We'd never ever let them forget that, that they were a bunch of thieves from the West of Scotland!

So, we had a lot of fun and the sense that the camaraderie in the band might be growing felt very real. I was coming out of a dark place and just beginning to get a sense of purpose again. I was still living in the house in Kensington. The distance between Stuart and myself was more than geographic now. It was quite a chasm. We were leading very, very different lives. He had got a mortgage and a home and was thinking about a family, whereas my life was still completely itinerant and had no formal structure to it. We arrived in the studio space and we knocked out the set for the upcoming tour pretty quickly. Russell and Mike had no problem picking up the songs and it was pretty easy to go through them, so we had a whole week left to do stuff. When we used to do John Peel sessions, or when we still did John Peel sessions at that point in time, instead of doing songs from the album, we actually used to arrive at the studio and just write new songs on the day, and we loved doing that. It was exciting and crazy and inventive and we felt liberated and free. I'm sure our record company hated us for doing it because they wanted us to promote the material that was about to come out. But we always used the time for our own benefit. So we decided instead of spending any more time rehearsing the set, that we would start writing new material. We knocked around a few ideas. It was all very dark. The new songs had a really experimental side to them, as well as the usual anthemic quality.

They were very, very intense lyrics inspired by Albert Camus, Jean Paul Sartre, Joy Division, Lou Reed, and Patti Smith. The title I gave the work we were doing was *Strength through Joy*, which was meant to be ironic, if you read the lyrics of the songs, they're ferociously anti- fascist and anti-totalitarianism. They have a sense of the individual's right against the collective and the focus on the individual's isolation and obviously this was a subject matter I kept on returning to. Then Stuart did his usual vanishing act. This time I think he may have given us a bit of warning that he wanted to go home for a couple of days.

Russell, Mike and myself started to note down some ideas and I'd been playing guitar now for quite a while on live stuff. Stuart had pretty much taught me to play so on the recordings we were doing I suddenly found myself trying a few things. It wasn't terrible, these very gentle loops, like on our tracks 'Snakes and Ladders' and 'A Man for all Seasons'. These new, slightly ambient things we were trying out. I spoke to Simon Draper and told him what we were doing. Literally within a few hours the mobile recording studio they had access to turned up and we started to record this stuff.

We told Stuart about it by phone and he said he'd be back down in a couple of days, so we just got on with it. We started to record these really elegant, elegiac, quite melancholy little ambient feeling, non-song-like experiments and they just worked, really beautifully, I think. 'Snakes and Ladders' is a lovely melancholic piece of music and 'A Man for all Seasons' could work beautifully in any film to do with landscapes. So we laid all these things down and then Stuart reappeared. I was certain he was going to hate them, and was going to be furious that we'd taken the design of the music of the band in this crazy direction without him being present and that he'd been betrayed in some way. I was expecting the worst when he arrived back, but, in fact, it was the complete opposite.

He couldn't believe that I had managed to play guitar with any proficiency in a recording studio and do something as sweet and simple as 'Snakes and Ladders' and 'A Man for all Seasons' and he immediately got creative. It was almost like he'd gone back to Scotland, got himself recharged, came back feeling excited about it after he heard what we had done, and then suddenly he really got involved with it — this little fun experimental thing we were trying. We only had a couple of days to record all this stuff and mix it down, but it was beginning to really work in a different way. And Stuart was great. He really got excited by working on tracks like 'An Incident in Algiers', 'Filming in Africa', 'A Man for all Seasons', 'Snakes and Ladders'. 'Surgical Triumph' is one of his inventions and 'The Bell Jar'.

So he really upped his game in a different way. Not the usual Stuart Adamson guitar lines. They were something you might associate with Robert Fripp or even the new Bill Nelson from Red Noise. It was really exciting and that experience became a free album that came with *The Absolute Game*. Out of what was supposed to be a rehearsal for the tour, actually we ended up creating a second album, as we prepared for that album's release and, obviously, the tour that would come with it, which we were all aware was a level we had never played before.

The idea that The Skids from Dunfermline could sell out one of the most iconic venues in the world, the Hammersmith Odeon was truly exciting and beyond that, the tour was going to end up in Edinburgh at my favourite venue, the Odeon, so it was something that gave me a reason for living... I think.

Into The Valley

CHAPTER TWENTY-SEVEN

I had become really good friends with Steve Severin from Siouxsie and the Banshees. We had originally met around at John McGeoch's house in Notting Hill Gate at a drinks event and we just immediately hit it off. I told him that I was a big fan of the Banshees and their adventurous approach to their music. I loved all their cinema and literary references and how they didn't really give a shit what anybody thought about them. I think most people would never have expected us to become such close friends, but we did. This was just at the time I had returned back from working on and completing *The Absolute Game* and the free album that would go with it.

So, just before the release of the album and the on- going tour, I did something completely crazy. I moved from the stability of having a warm, decent, clean home in Kensington Mews to moving into a flat with Severin up in Priory Road in West Hampstead, in a damp basement. It really became party central. It was a crazy environment and the Banshees had a very close knit group of friends which went from some of the people that followed the band, who worked with the band, or other musicians that they felt they had something akin to. Like Robert Smith from the Cure and journalists like Paul Morley from the *New Musical Express* who were regulars around Priory Road at these crazy parties Severin would just organise out of the blue.

In the flat itself, we spent a lot of time watching movies, listening to music, and going to the cinema. Cinema seemed to be the daily diet of our life; jump in a taxi to the Scala near Tottenham Road to watch a Tarkovsky movie, like *Stalker*, or go to the Gate Cinema in Notting Hill to watch a Dirk Bogarde movie like *Night Porter*. Every night seemed to have something going on, but it could be a book reading, an art gallery, a different movie, or just hanging out in this very close-knit bunch of people who I had suddenly been adopted by. Of course, this wasn't drawing me any closer to even considering moving back to Scotland. It was actually drawing me further away, but it was exciting to be with a lot of like minded people who had shared my love of German art and literature.

Steve was very aware of my health condition. I told him that from the beginning. He seemed to look out for me and we had a really good time in that crazy flat. I became very close to Siouxsie and Budgie and Robert Smith who was working with them at that point in time. But he was about to be replaced with McGeoch, because he had to go off and work with his own band, the Cure. So it was a really incredible time, full of young people with vibrant ideas with a really sound sense of who they were and where they were headed in life and who didn't really take any shit from anyone.

I was still doing my performances in the Cabaret Futura. The Banshees and the gang used to come down and shout abuse at me as I stood up on stage reading versions of my take on *India Song* by Marguerite Duras. Or, again, every week I would do a performance of *Daddy* by Sylvia Plath, which was a pretty crazy piece of work and quite theatrical. It was at one of these evenings that a young playwright,

Chris Ward, came and spoke to me about becoming involved in his new play, which was called *Demonstration of Affection*. He wanted to do a short run in a small theatre just off Marleybone Road and would I be willing to play this crazy young punk guy in the play, because he felt there was something theatrical about my performances that might work.

I still had that same attitude of well, why not, I'll give it a go, what have you got to lose? Time is not on my side, so just go for it. So I did a brief period before the big tour started. We had one more set of rehearsals in Scotland before we started, so I had a couple of weeks where I had a go at being on stage as an actor during this crazy, insane period, which got a lot of attention. I'm not sure that it was very good, but I certainly enjoyed participating and it was great to work with the other actors who were all young and from different social backgrounds. It wasn't my idea of what the theatre was about. I always thought it was a bit of a rarefied, bourgeois world, but this didn't seem to be the case.

The play was a big success. People came to see it in quite large numbers. It was sold out most nights and my friends came. I remember Steve Jones and Paul Cook from the Sex Pistols actually shouting at me when I came onstage about how shit I was and even the Banshees came and laughed their socks off at my performance, although everybody from the theatre world said it wasn't so terrible. I was asked by certain agencies if I'd be interested in taking this more seriously, but at the time I didn't really want to advance on it. It was just a new experience that I wanted to sample and, of course, I had this big tour where the Skids would be playing the biggest dates they'd ever played coming up, so I had to get my head around that.

But it was good fun and I enjoyed it and I certainly

parked the idea that it might be something to return to. In the meantime, the social life around Priory Road was insane and I remember waking up one day and Kris Needs, who was a journalist who hung out with the Banshees, was tied to the tree at the bottom of the garden. He'd been sitting out there all night and he was still asleep.

I went out and came back and he was still there, until I eventually untied the poor guy. There was a lot of strange things going on there. Steve enjoyed the company of many different women at the time and I was very envious of his ability to charm the living daylights out of people, because I was a bit quieter when it came to the opposite sex, although very noisy when I was in a group. Everybody seemed to think I was a natural performer, but actually, underneath it all, I was a very shy person.

CHAPTER TWENTY-EIGHT

Were we as ambitious for *The Absolute Game* tour as we had been for the *Days in Europa* tour? In musical terms, yes, but in production terms, no. It was much more of a straightforward rock 'n' roll tour, playing big venues, and we had taken on another new management team. Ian Grant and Alan Edwards were a partnership we had met previously when we had toured with The Stranglers. They had been The Stranglers' management and had been around the music scene for quite a while.

I principally got on very well with Alan Edwards, I thought he was a great guy and easy to talk to. We both had a soft spot for Arsenal football team and would go there together often, whereas I always found Ian Grant a little bit trickier. I never really quite felt I knew where I was with him, and he seemed much closer to Stuart than I, but with Alan, I felt the connection. At least we had management in place, which made Virgin Records happier, before we embarked on our biggest tour to date. My initial idea for the production was to have film footage being shown behind us again, but it was proving to be financially difficult to do that and there was no sense that we needed to do it with this tour because the general feeling was that the album was so strong. It had been received very well both critically and commercially. It was felt we just needed to get out there and let the songs do the talking. It was a tour playing the major cities of the UK and Ireland, and each and every one of them, really, had their own special qualities.

The standout cities remain with me to this day. Belfast was probably one of the highlights, I really loved playing Belfast and always do. Because the Skids come from both sides of the sectarian divide, there was never any question of tribalism when the band played in the city. People were very thankful that we had made the effort to come, and we always had an enormous crowd. Gigs were always sold out when we played there, and the response was overwhelming. That proved to be the case again during this particular tour.

All of the various cities we played in England and Scotland had high points, and the general sense was that the set we had put together, which was the longest we'd ever played on stage, really had a lot of nice dynamic qualities. Playing songs from *Scared to Dance* and *Days in Europa*, but the majority of the material still came from *The Absolute Game* — the obvious ones, of course, like 'Circus Game', 'Hurry On Boys', 'Goodbye Civilian' and 'Happy to be With You'.

But we also played songs like 'Arena', that was a little bit more complex but for me a very richly emotional song, and I loved performing it on that tour. It was my highlight of the evening when we got to that point in time, and screaming the repeated anthemic words at the end, that "all the boys are innocent and lonely." The big gig of course was when we got to London, playing Hammersmith Odeon. At that point in time, I got the feeling from Stuart that he was much happier with the combination of Russell and Mike, he felt more secure with them musically.

The performances up to that point had been uproarious and we had an energy that we'd never had before.

We even found new levels to physically take the music to on stage. There's a wonderful picture by Virginia Turbett of Adamson flying in one direction and I'm flying in another direction, and that was *The Absolute Game* tour, which really captured the joyfulness of the band. We seemed to be in a good place. The commercial value of the band was still high, people felt that this was a breakthrough album, that we had found our touch again in the sense of it being much more of a rock 'n' roll album than an experimental album.

We had put all the experimental stuff on the free album that came with it, which people seemed to like very much. When we got to the day of playing Hammersmith Odeon, of course we were in a state of dizzy excitement. This is probably one of the most iconic gigs in the world and and there we were. For some reason, Stuart disappeared again on the day of the gig. He hadn't told us where he was going, nobody could contact him, nobody could find him.

We got to the soundcheck around 4:30, and he hadn't been in touch with anyone. He didn't show up for the soundcheck, and we started to think we were going to have to cancel the gig. The biggest gig of our lives and he just hadn't bothered showing up. It was not unusual of course, because we'd been going through this on so many different occasions, but come on, not on this particular day. We tried to keep it quiet so the record company or the promoter didn't know. We just said he wasn't feeling very well and he'd gone back to the hotel, but we had absolutely no idea where he was, and he certainly wasn't at the hotel.

Russell, Mike, and myself went through the motions at the soundcheck, but we felt a sense of gloom and disappointment, being let down by him yet again on this particular day of days. Then as the evening unfolded, the support band went on and played, and there was still no sign of Adamson. The clock was ticking away, it was maybe 8:30 and we were on stage at nine, and he showed up with about ten minutes to go. He didn't apologise to anyone, he didn't say a word. We just got on stage.

It was one of the great Skids performances. I think the other members of the band, including myself, felt so angry that we were being treated this way by him that we just put in a physical, angry performance that caught all the songs in a very particular way — gave them an edge and a dynamic quality that they already had but we pushed them to another level. That was really as a response and a reaction to the disparaging way we were being treated by Adamson and his attitude to us, that any minor unhappiness meant everybody else had to pay for it.

This was at the stage when Ian Grant and Alan Edwards actually really genuinely felt that they could take the Skids to a higher level — push us into America for sure, and they had already started to position us to do some gigs in New York straight after the tour, which we were all excited about. But they had just been given their first taste of the disappearing act of Stuart Adamson as he vanished off into his own world. In later years, of course, I spoke to other people who had worked with him after me, and that pattern never changed, it continued until the day he died. He had dark things that he carried around with him.

Some of them I was aware of, not all of them of course, and I wasn't really familiar with some of the detail of what was going on in his head, but certainly I knew the cause of some of his distress. But he showed great disdain for his fellow band members and what we were about.

After the Hammersmith Odeon, which was a phenomenal success, the feeling about the band had grown higher and higher, but I think it was the Hammersmith Odeon that made me think that the project might be doomed, that this guy was getting worse. That he could do something so drastic on the day of the biggest gig of our lives was a real shock to me.

I had been at the coalface with him from the very beginning, and I know I had begun to irritate the shit out of him because of the fact that I was very much part of the London scene and I was hanging out with Severin and the Banshees gang. We just felt really distant from one another. It was impossible to talk about these things other than in a superficial way, and I actually almost had to talk through Sandra, to try and coerce some information out, to work out what the hell was going on. And it was difficult to work out what was going on.

In the context of my own life, it was becoming really exhausting to get a sense of where we might be within twenty-four hours. But there was definitely an air of gloom that I didn't share with anyone else, because I didn't want to jeopardise the tour — that the Skids might be slowly but surely unwinding and coming to an end, and the reason they'd be coming to an end is because he had lost his sense of purpose in the band or maybe even lost his sense of purpose with life. The tour continued after the Odeon gig, and we had tried to have some fun with the rest of it. Which was very difficult considering what had happened.

The other spectacular night was the return to the Odeon in Edinburgh, and I remember on that day I'd lost my voice. I was totally exhausted and feeling physically in a mess and didn't really want to perform but obviously was going to carry on. I couldn't find my voice, it just wouldn't work at the soundcheck, and we got out to do the opening song, which I think was 'Animation' still, and nothing happened, it just wasn't there. I had to physically drag my voice out from the back of my throat for the whole of the gig.

But a little bit like the Hammersmith Odeon gig, it gave me an energy that I never knew I had. I was like a whirling dervish that evening, jumping through the air, doing backflips and spinning, and it was a combination of frustration — that I couldn't get my voice to work like I wanted it to and also the anger I felt. That all the things I'd put myself through mentally, physically, psychologically to continue with the band and support Adamson were in my mind coming to an end. I could really feel it, and the way he just didn't want to communicate in the way that he used to.

Everything was very polite and cordial but something was amiss. Even straight after the tour, we jumped on a plane and went to New York. This should have been, like the Hammersmith Odeon gig, a really special moment in our lives. But it wasn't, he wasn't interested, and he didn't really want to be there, he wanted to be with Sandra. They went off together in New York, didn't hang out with the rest of us, just left us to get on with it, which was another clear sign that this was definitely going in the wrong direction.

I'm not sure that Russell and Mike were so aware of this, although there was actually a tension brewing between them as well. Russell was always pushing Mike, because Russell had a very high regard for himself as a musician and as a songwriter. he didn't think Mike was up to it, which is complete bullshit, because Mike's performance on The Absolute Game is one of the outstanding things on the record, alongside Stuart's guitar playing, and his melodies. Russell's musicianship is pretty good but he does nothing exceptional, whereas the other two did exceptional work on that record.

You could see that Mike was a very soft, gentle guy who was being bullied by Russell, and it was having an effect. Maybe Stuart saw all these things and thought he was losing a grasp of the musical direction of the band, because Russell started to make himself more vocal about where we should be headed and he wanted more to do with the songwriting. Invariably I feel that, that had a massive effect on Stuart. As well as the feeling that I was cast adrift in a strange world that he didn't want to be part of. Stuart looked down his nose and was quite scathing about the whole London scene. He had no ambition to be part of that kind of thing, he wanted to be in his beloved home and have a family life.

None of these things were of any interest to me, I still didn't even really have a proper relationship at that point in time. It's ironic, but at the end of the *Absolute Game* tour and coming home from New York, the band should have been feeling like the world was at their feet, because it was an amazing place we were at, selling out every gig we played and audiences going crazy because of these physical and richly emotional performances, but in fact it was the opposite. That sense of doom and gloom was truly apparent to me as I stepped off the flight back from New York and landed back in London.

Into The Valley

CHAPTER TWENTY-NINE

At the end of the *Absolute Game* tour I left the cavalcade of a touring band feeling that something wasn't right. The tour had been an amazing success and we had played to the biggest audiences ever. The new music had been heralded by our growing fan base. So, we were at the peak of our powers and probably one of the best live bands of our generation. The music really came alive on stage in a way that a lot of bands couldn't compete with.

So, we were in a position of strength and things from the outside looked like we were to become a really successful band on an international scale. But there was something a little bit dark lying at the back of my head because the Hammersmith Odeon debacle had left a bad taste in my mouth. It had suggested something was much deeper in Adamson's wayward behaviour.

The idea that you turn up ten minutes before you go on stage at the biggest gig of your life is nothing to do with nerves that's to do with something going on in your own life that you're not happy with. You're not happy with the band, you're not happy with the people in the band; you've got stuff going on from your own family history that's tormenting you. A combination of all of those things drove that guy to behave in the way he did. But of course the responsibility for his feelings also lies at my doorstep because he must have been looking at me and thinking where is his value system, what happens to the value system that we both cherished? Even politically we were both big Labour supporting socialists whose views were very much of the left. There I was running around London like some dandy having a party every night, through his eyes at least, with my new found friends. Playing the part of some two dollar rock star, loving the press attention, going off and doing plays and spoken word records so randomly without a plan.

From the outside it must have looked like I had become a complete and utter wanker to him. And why didn't I want what he wanted? Why had I even lost the Skids value system of just improving our music and focusing on the music and everything else is irrelevant? Whereas it was almost like the only thing that was relevant in my mind was having a good time and being out there, being seen and trying new things and in his eyes probably being very, very pretentious. He had a mortgage, a wife, starting a family — that's how he saw the world.

Looking at me he would have seen this crazy guy just running around randomly doing stuff, wasn't involved in a relationship, couldn't concentrate anymore just wanted to be part of a scene and that scene was in London or over in mainland Europe. So, through his eyes it must have become very frustrating and disappointing but he'd forgotten what I'd told him at the beginning of our friendship that I would grasp everything by the horns and shake it because I felt I might not be around that long.

He knew that so I don't know if he had conveniently forgotten it or he thought that I had applied that state of mind through my behaviour in completely the wrong way. He may well have been right. On the relationship front I had lots of friends who were girls and I had one- night stands of course but never any deep relationship. Privately I hadn't said anything to the other members but I was starting to see somebody.

I'd met a girl called Mariella Frostrup who was around the same age as me and had the most incredible energy and warmth and she was a good person. She really understood that I was a little bit crazy and she put up with that. She understood that I'd come from a troubled background as she had herself I might add. She seemed to be able to put up with my self-indulgence and petulance and sometimes the darkness. She was aware that at nights I had these small minor attacks and that I didn't really know what to do about it and occasionally just looked incredibly ill.

None of this seemed to be a problem to Mariella and she was very accepting of what I was. I think I was a bit of a shit to her in the early days because I just wasn't sure I wanted to have a deeper, more meaningful relationship. I didn't really want to expose myself emotionally to anyone other than through the songs. So, I found that a very difficult hurdle to cross. However, slowly but surely through her patience and decency and I guess love, that started to change. I started to be more comfortable in her company and started to really enjoy being with her.

Whilst this was going on I got a phone call from Ian Grant to tell me that Stuart had decided to fire me from the band. The idea that I was no longer the singer in the Skids came as a shock to everybody apart from me. At the end of the *Absolute Game* tour I felt I saw something coming, something big. He no longer communicated with me and I think he held me in disdain although my performances on stage were better than they'd ever been. Certainly my inputs with the songs were as strong as they ever were.

But my position in the ideology of what the Skids

represented had probably faded in his eyes and he'd had enough of that dilettante and maybe he thought to steal something from our own songs was a bit of a charade. So it was time for us to part and he thought I should go. Ian Grant and Alan Edwards suggested that I go up to Edinburgh and sit down with Stuart and have a conversation about it at least. I thought it was a good idea because I was actually okay with the fact that he no longer wanted to work with me.

But at least we should end where we began as friends not as enemies. I checked into a really ugly hotel in the St James Centre and was told that he would call me. I was there for three days and I made it clear, I left a message at his home, saying where I was and gave him all the details and waited. But nothing came. At the end of the third day I'd had enough of waiting and I really felt like I'd had enough of being treated this way by him so that was it.

I called Grant and Edwards to say I was leaving. They said just hang on one minute, let's make one last call. They obviously had spoken to him and they called me back and said, "oh, no, everything's fine he thinks he was just going through a strange moment in his head. He wants to get together in the next few weeks and start working on material for the next Skids album." I said, "well is he not going to speak to me directly and maybe apologise?" They said "I think not so I just think you should let it go, everything's fine and get on with your life. We'll start preparing for you guys to get together and create new material over the next few weeks or month."

And that was it, no apology, no letter, no nothing just, yes, everything's fine. A little bit like the Hammersmith Odeon turning up ten minutes before we go on stage to the biggest gig of our lives. Oh, yes, everything's fine; just forget about what just happened. It's pretty exhausting stuff and I started to feel that deeply. It made my health feel really deleterious, I felt really anxious and I really did not feel very well at all, both physically and mentally.

I went back to London that day and in the evening I went to a Polanski double bill in the Holborn area of London. It was *China Town* and *The Tenant*. During the movie I was feeling really ill, my heart was racing and I knew something was up. I didn't say anything to Russell who went with me. I started to feel like I was going to pass out. But we got through China Town an amazing piece of work but I couldn't really concentrate on the screen. When The Tenant started a combination of the music and just the strangeness of that film started to really affect me and I started to feel even worse.

I decided to go to the foyer and call Mariella and say can I come over to your place because I'm not feeling very good. That's all I remember. I woke up and I was in a hospital and I had very worried doctors looking at me. I'd had a minor heart attack through a seizure, an epileptic seizure that had lasted too long and my heart had really been affected very badly by that. It was an extraordinary moment because I'd just come through the turbulence of being fired from the band that I had created and loved and nurtured, by my strange creative partner.

I think that, amongst many other things, compounded my well-being and I had this full blown seizure which was the worst I'd ever had. Normally my seizures happen during the night. They're called absence seizures and make me have quite sleepless nights. This was the first time that I'd had a big one during normal hours and the effect was disastrous.

Afterwards I felt really weak and I had so many other little things to do before we started work on the new Skids project. I'd promised my friend Julian Sands, an actor who was also a director, that I would do a one-week performance with him and his group of actors in the Auden/Isherwood play, *The Dog Beneath the Skin* down at the Mile End Theatre. It was only a week's run and I had done some rehearsals for the play previously. It was only a small part I was playing and so it was nothing significant. But I had promised to do it.

I'd also agreed to do an adaptation of Marguerite Duras', *10.30 on a Summer Night*. I was supposed to go to Brussels to do that but I just couldn't face it. To top all that off the Crépuscule had released my first ever book of poetry called *A Man for All Seasons*. So, in a typical way that my life was conducted, these things just came from everywhere at the same time.

Actually that has never changed. That still happens to this day, work just comes pouring out all at the same time. There's no sense of structure to it, it's just that the impulse to make it and get it out there is stronger than the more strategic thinking of is this a good thing to do at this moment in time? I never think that way I just want to do stuff. So, I'm much less cynical than people might imagine about the work that I have created.

So I agreed even though I was very sick. I did the play in which I was terrible because I just wasn't well. On the days off Mariella actually had helped put some musicians together to help me record in a small studio in Fulham. I recorded the *10.30 on a Summer Night;* it was done in a day, the whole thing. Spoken word records were always done in a day or half a day, they didn't take long, I was always relatively well prepared for them.

So, I left this period of instability that I had of being fired then rehired with a massive physical and mental attack health wise. But I still managed to be in a play and record a spoken work record and release my first ever book. It was a pretty crazy time as I got the word from Ian Grant and Alan Edwards that the rehearsal for the next Skids material would happen in Inverness in a rehearsal space and then we would record some demos. The idea was that with these new demos we would work again with Bill Nelson. I felt that maybe that was what Stuart wanted because he would be working again with somebody he had so much respect for.

Maybe we would turn a corner in our evolution and it would also help with our relationship. I was concerned before I got there because of what had gone on before but it was another new Skids chapter so there was a modicum of excitement. However, not too much this time, unfortunately.

Into The Valley

CHAPTER THIRTY

Before we left for the studio in Inverness, we rehearsed in Dunfermline. This was the first time Stuart and I had been together since he had told me he no longer wanted me in the band. It had that usual Stuart Adamson clumsiness at the beginning of the sessions, but we decided just to get on with it. The feeling at this point in time was that maybe we could push on the sound into something unique. Maybe something that nobody else had done and, or even considered. There was a sense of folk music being at the heart of a lot of the Skids tunes and Stuart had a deep love of Scotland and its traditions. In a way it felt natural really to take these songs back to where they really came from.

We started to play around with different ideas. It was very confusing because in some ways we wanted to take our sound into what was happening in the world around us; musically, at least. People were trying to make sure that their songs could work in a club and on the radio, but still have an edge and not lose it. It's something we had tried in *Days in Europa*, with Rusty Egan and the drum sequences.

There were a few songs we started to play around with that might have that rhythm, but at the same time, this idea of doing something folksy was at the heart of it. I'd written an idea called 'Iona', which felt like a ballad. It didn't really move along at any particular pace when we were in this rehearsal space, and without realising, I think Russell saw that there was a chasm between Stuart and I in the way that we wrote together in the past to the way we were then.

There was definitely a problem there. I'm not sure if it was cynical or not, but he simply moved into that space. I don't really know why I let it happen, but he suddenly wanted to take the lyrics of 'Iona' that I was playing around with and do them himself, because he felt he was a stronger songwriter. This is the first time this had ever happened in the Skids — that somebody had come in and said I'm writing the songs now. It was a real shock to Stuart and I, but our relationship had deteriorated so much that neither of us fought it. In retrospect, of course, we should have said "no, absolutely no fucking way", but we allowed Webb to come in with his lyrics, which are terrible. I hate the song 'Iona', it's just awful. It's an embarrassingly lame, stupid song. The lyrics are idiotic and it's something I really never want to be associated with. It's got none of the things that I feel embody the Skids.

It's just a soft piece of sentimental mush that has no meaning and it's ridiculous that we allowed it to happen. But that's how bad the relationship was. Webb had his eye on something, maybe his own reflection, that he wanted to make it his song. There was still a part of me that had this thing of trying to make Stuart happy during these periods, although in this particular occasion maybe less so, after what I'd been through and my energy level was still quite low. I just wasn't sure where this might be going. Normally, we entered the writing phase of a new album with real anticipation and excitement of where we could take the band's sound and where I could take my lyrics to, but this felt different, and certainly the example of allowing Webb to step in and take over the song 'Iona' proves beyond any doubt that my relationship with Stuart was not in a good place. Russell was still also treating Mike as if he was incapable of stepping up to the plate and he really made him feel like a lesser person behind the scenes. Sometimes he couldn't stop himself. He did it in front of everybody, which was humiliating for Mike. Mike was quite a gentle soul, a really nice guy, and really, in the end, had, had enough. He walked out of the rehearsal space one day and never came back. I've spoken to Mike about what happened and, in his eyes, it was a combination of many things, but essentially he felt the band was going nowhere after the amazing success of *The Absolute Game* and that incredible tour where I thought Mike was brilliant. Something to be proud of.

Suddenly it was all over the place, even management-wise, Ian Grant and Alan Edwards weren't doing anything really with us. We thought they could have taken us to another level with The Absolute Game but they hadn't done and we were just back in the cycle of writing again without feeling we had advanced beyond the UK. The other thing at that time which still shocks me, was we were all broke. We had no money, even though I had signed a decent publishing deal. We shared all of the songs with parity and equal writing credits on *The Absolute Game*, but none of us had made any money. Stuart probably being the wisest of all of us had gotten himself a home and a mortgage and probably was more settled, but we were all pretty much strapped for cash.

Mike reflected on the whole scheme of things and had also had enough of Russell, who could be a really nasty piece of work. I often question myself how... why did I stay working with that guy, because he's not the kind of person that I'd ever want to be in company with. I don't regard him as a friend. I don't regard him as a creative ally. In fact, I ended up regarding him as an enemy, somebody I disliked tremendously, and would never spend any time with, even to this day.

So, we moved on to Inverness without a drummer. Russell suggested bringing in his friend from The Zones, Kenny Hyslop, who was obviously a good drummer, but he'd been going through a lot of troubles himself, but he played with us up in Inverness in front of Bill Nelson, who came to oversee the production and we knocked around a few songs.

One was 'Brave Man'. Kenny does his bit of disco drumming on that track, and, of course, 'Iona'. Bill didn't like either of the songs and he had a very negative view of the way that Russell was dominating the whole production, like he had taken charge and Stuart didn't seem to be interested anymore. We were on the outskirts of the town in an outlying area which felt quite isolated. We thought it might be the right environment to record these new folksy songs, but that wasn't what was happening. Songs like 'Brave Man' had a different kind of feel, but we talked about how we could make 'Blood and Soil' fit into this new style of music that we were trying to create.

But it just didn't seem to gel, nothing seemed to gel. It was very clumsy. Bill Nelson actually walked out of the recording, feeling that he couldn't contribute anything. That was entirely due to the fact that he felt Stuart and I weren't that interested and we'd allowed Russell to take control. We had, because he then took on the mantle of the producer of 'Iona', which was his song, from my idea. Stuart and I just hated the song. It was just awful. I think there was a little moment where we watched all of the years of hard work, all of the things we had achieved together, all of the dreams that had come true, and all of the failures we had created, were just all there in front of us.

Into The Valley

I think there was a little moment in Inverness where we caught each other's eye and felt maybe this was it and the sessions were not going very well. The loss of Nelson, was obviously an embarrassment to us and suddenly I felt Stuart was gone. He had never really been present in those sessions and my instincts told me this time that the game was up. He went off home and left Inverness without saying anything, but my feeling about the whole thing was not good. The dereliction of duty on our part, Stuart and I, of allowing somebody else to come in and command the sound of the band, something that we have created, something that was ours, our energy, our music, our force, our vision, somebody to come in and just ruin that with this idiotic, stupid song was a killer.

In retrospect, of course, I take absolute responsibility for allowing that to happen. I introduced that person to the band and I didn't fight it. I could've fought it and I didn't. I didn't fight it because I just didn't have the will at the time and I just felt maybe a little lost myself again and maybe I'd stopped caring. It was difficult to know, really. I was still probably seething from having been kicked out and then rehired, so to speak, but not even a word had been said about it when we were rehearsing in Dunfermline and working up in Inverness. But there was no doubt that during that session I wasn't present and neither was Stuart.

We allowed somebody else, who didn't really understand the connection that Stuart and I had, to take control and therefore, the Skids, as we had known them, the Skids that created 'Charles' and the No Bad Label, the Skids that had created *Scared to Dance* and 'Into the Valley' and the 'Saints are Coming', and the Skids who had created 'Masquerade' and the beautiful record, *Days in Europa*, with all of its different complexities, and the beginnings of the energy of *The Absolute Game*, had gone. It wasn't there anymore and it was clear, really, to Stuart and to me that what we had was over and we'd never get it back. The distance, geographically, between us had created a cultural chasm that we just couldn't fill. The connection had been broken.

The sense of honour and integrity was fractured and the responsibility of making sure that the music was the key to what we were about was no longer present, so from his point of view it was finished. I also understood, I think, at that point in time, the journey The Skids had been on up until that time was completely over.

There was a responsibility to carry on with the recording, but my feeling was maybe we needed to take a break and then rethink the project, speak to Virgin about it, but I knew what was going to happen next and, of course, it did. We got a phone call the next day saying that Stuart had left the band. He no longer wanted anything to do with the band and he wanted nothing to do with the current recordings and he was going to go off and do his own thing and that was it.

Now, normally, because this had happened so many times before, I would be put in the position where I had to go running after him and chasing him to find out what lay underneath that statement and, in some way, convince him that maybe if we changed a few things he could get the band that he once loved back again. But I knew it was over, so there was no point, and no matter how much people like Grant and Edwards told me you've got to speak to him, I knew there was no point, because I didn't really want him back this time. I wanted him to just go and get on with his life and be happy and have children and get a new band together and be successful. I never, at any point in time, felt any antipathy towards Stuart.

I have always retained my respect for him to this day. I

was delighted with the success he had with Big Country. I was so happy for him when he had two children, because that's what he always wanted, he wanted to be a father and he had lovely kids, and never did I feel anger about it, maybe a little frustration, of course, but no anger, no antipathy, no bitterness.

I felt responsible for the Skids coming to an end and that saddens me in many ways, so I left Inverness and went back to London, not a broken person, but essentially I had been on this incredible journey and it had come to an end. I needed to rethink everything about who I was, what I was, what I wanted to do, and where I was going to go from there. Was this it? The one thing the Skids hadn't done was make me financially wealthy or stable, but maybe what it had given me was a platform and an opportunity to explore ideas and try and be brave with the creative process. And I will be forever thankful for that.

Into The Valley

CHAPTER THIRTY-ONE

With Stuart Adamson gone everything seemed upside down. How do you continue? What is it that you're part of now? Even the organisation around us, the management of Ian Grant and Alan Edwards seemed to be less and less involved and he's the one that I actually got on with. Ian Grant seemed to be a hindrance and he decided, off his own back, to continue working with Stuart. We went to Virgin Records and explained the situation, that there was no way back with Adamson. It was over. They wanted us to do some more demos of the new material. They'd obviously heard 'Iona' and felt, with a bit of help, it could be maybe made into a more commercial record, and they involved Mike Oldfield, which just seemed so ridiculous. I think about our punk origins and here we were, working with this trippy hippy, Mike Oldfield, the man with the multimillion selling *Tubular Bells* behind him.

But he did bring something very sweet to the song, but there's no two ways around it, I just didn't like the song. It had nothing to do with the Skids. It was a piece of mush. I regretted ever coming up with the idea and I certainly regret ever allowing Russell Webb the space to turn the song into some sentimental crap. There was one song that we had come up with, that I felt was still in the spirit of the Skids. It was folksy and tough and had an edge and had an anthemic chorus and that was called 'Fields'. Virgin agreed to us going into a studio with a guy called Mike Hodges and we started to record the backing track for 'Fields'. Mike had been working with a Scottish band, the Associates, which were lead by the wonderful Billy McKenzie, who had become a very dear friend of mine.

I asked Billy if he would come down and do the backing vocals on 'Fields', just to give it something special in the sense of how Stuart Adamson's harmonies and very sweet voice used to give the Skids another very beautiful layer in the polished finished songs. Billy did the most incredible one take that I've ever heard in my experience of being in studios. It was just magic. Mike Hodges was a great engineer who put up with Russell Webb's bullshit, who had taken the role as producer, again, with no fight from me.

I really put the success of the sound of 'Fields' down to Hodges and also Billy McKenzie doing the most astonishing backing vocal. 'Fields' was the closest thing we were in that whole project which was to be called Joy, that was close to what my idea of where we could've progressed the Skids to, when we were rehearsing in Dunfermline and then recording in Inverness. But, of course, that never happened, because we focused on the wrong material.

Virgin was excited by the possibilities of where this might be going because of 'Fields', so we were put into a studio in Islington in North London with Russell Webb as producer, which was a disastrous decision, to record an album that would be called *Joy*. The people involved in the album were very mixed, came from different types of groups and, in all honesty, it's a blur to me now, because I didn't enjoy the experience very much and the strange arrangements of some of the songs were difficult for me to sing. In some way, Stuart always wrote songs in a key that suited my voice. Russell seemed to write songs that were almost impossible to try and sing. It was right at my limit and he thought that was great, you've got to push yourself further, but you're just managing to get through it rather than give it any emotion or richness or complexity.

I found the whole recording process of *Joy* a disappointment. I thought with 'Fields' maybe there was somewhere we could go that would be really special, but Russell didn't have the touch that Stuart had. He didn't have the magic, he didn't have the ability to take my lyrics and turn them into anthems and choruses that people would want to sing along with. He was just a different type of musician, he was a very good musician, he was very strong, and I'm sure, with more experience, he would've become a better producer, but that album, apart from 'Fields' and maybe 'Blood and Soil', does not feel like a Skids album. Obviously, Stuart's not on the album and these songs feel like they're missing him, but they're missing the Skids. It's not even Stuart Adamson, it's the Skids, it's the rush. The lines are all in there, the volley and thunder, where is it, you know?

Apart from, as I say, 'Fields' and 'Blood and Soil', I

just can't hear it. I listen to the album sometimes as an album that's got nothing to do with the concept of the Skids and it's okay, it feels okay. It's got some really nice moments on it and I feel, lyrically at least, I've got something to be proud of in that record, but the idea that we gave it the title *Joy* by the Skids is wrong. I think it should've been something new and therefore, we would've been able to relax into it more. Or I certainly would've been able to relax into it more, like I did when, eventually, this was over and I started the Armoury Show. I was very relaxed about that project and I was much more protective of my own place,

Into The Valley

because I knew what I was up against with this guy, Webb. But certainly, during *Joy,* I don't think my heart was in it as a Skids project.

As a set of ideas that should've been called something else other than the Skids or by somebody else other than the Skids, then yes, I can feel some great things in there, but Russell Webb didn't really understand the Skids without the guidance of Stuart Adamson and I really felt his loss as we moved through that album. Strangely enough if you listen to 'Fields' and then you listen to early Big Country, you can feel there's a connection, there's something going on between what we were doing with 'Fields' and what he did with Big Country that suggested, if we had got focused up there in Inverness on the right things with the right guidance and probably with the right producer, and Bill Nelson was the wrong producer for that material and Russell Webb was also definitely the wrong producer, then we may have found something.

We may have found the key. What Stuart and I should've done, really, when we sat down together to work, before we went to Inverness, is probably get rid of Russell and just start to rebuild the band in the way that he wanted it to be, the way that he felt the direction of the music should be going in, without having people trampling all over him. But, of course, easy things to say in retrospect. Would I have continued with the Skids? Would it have got stronger? I don't think so. I think *The Absolute Game* tour and that moment at Hammersmith Odeon really was the end. The end just got delayed and working on these new songs in Inverness was just a delaying tactic to see if we could pull another rabbit out of the hat. But this time we weren't able to.

So, *Joy* is an album that has got a lot of high points, but it's not a Skids album in my mind and, although I listen to it now and enjoy it, I don't enjoy it as a Skids album. The connection between what we could've done if it continued along the line of 'Fields', which had that commercial edge, although it was punk folk, was exactly what Stuart did when he evolved into the blossoming music of Big Country. Certainly for the first album, which was a tremendous success for the band. And, I repeat, I wished him well.

We did meet on many occasions after, when he had big success with Big Country and we always got on very well. I had visited him in Dunfermline at his home with Sandra and his kids, and never felt any acrimony whatsoever. I only felt a sense of happiness for him that he got what he thought he wanted. At the end of the *Joy* debacle, it was clear it was over. The album came out and it got very negative responses from critics who didn't understand it or didn't want to understand it. They thought it was pretentious gobbledygook and we had lost our way. The signposting, the semiotics of the Skids was the lighthouse that was the music of Stuart Adamson, and without him there we were incapable of recreating that sound.

I think there's a lot of truth in that. I think in life you have to accept defeat gracefully, something I've managed to do many times, because I do so many different types of things, which I enjoy immensely. But a lot of them have been immense failures that haven't really worked as well as I would've liked them to or haven't been appreciated critically or commercially and you accept it, but it doesn't stop you. You pick yourself up and you dust yourself down and you move on. So I had reached the end, the *Joy* album was the end of the Skids. And there was no way of taking it any further because it would've been a terrible lie. It would've been a lie to the people who had become our friends, the people that bought the records, who had a great sense of love for the band, so I couldn't do that. The one thing I've always tried to hold on to is a respect for the very people that followed us.

So, it was naturally time to close the book on the Skids at that moment in time. My own life was in the strangest of places. I was involved with Mariella and I was about to get married to her at such a young age. The marriage wouldn't last very long and that wasn't her fault. It was my fault because I was a person who was troubled, I was a person who instinctively needed to move around and do things that were constantly different, and I wasn't a detail person. Emotionally, I was a car crash, so what she had to put up with was beyond the call of duty, but I would say all I ever got back was warmth and kindness and generosity and maybe even a little bit of love.

So, again, sometimes in life you have to take responsibility and it was my fault that the relationship didn't work. But, again, like my friendship with Stuart Adamson, I retained that and I retained my friendship with my ex-wife, so there's no acrimony in any of these things. You've just got to accept responsibility that you were the person at the heart of these failings and you were responsible for not making a success of these things. So, there I was then, at the end of this incredible journey, with no band, single, and broke, and my health really not in the most wonderful place. And you think well, where can a person go from here? I had a lot of places in mind.

EPILOGUE

So much has happened in my life since the end of attempt to work with Russell Webb on a new project The Armoury Show. We had the brilliant John McGeoch in-between us to hopefully balance our sizeable egos. We signed with EMI and made a reasonable album *Waiting for The Floods*. Nothing happened. The world was not interested. McGeoch who was becoming increasingly soaked in booze and drugs
left to join PIL and I was left with Webb again. It would be reasonable to assume the project was fucked.

I did some more acting, this time with a political company, Paines Plough but found it hard going. My marriage was over. It probably never got started. I'll take the blame for that. I turned my back on music other than the odd spoken word project. A new book *16 Years of Alcohol* was released in 1986 which I performed around Europe, sometimes in the company of William Burroughs. During a performance in Paris I was asked to model for Commes des Garcon and suddenly my big face was all over the place. I was making money for the first time in my life. I continued to travel, east and west coast America and always back to Europe, especially Berlin.

On a trip back to the UK I was asked to audition for anew TV show. Why not? I got the job so was back in the

Into The Valley

UK presenting a show about the Arts in London. I still felt like I didn't fit in and my health was worse than ever. A doctor suggested I change the way I eat, sleep and live. Go to the gym, get healthy, fight back was the mantra and it worked I started to feel better, stronger and able to control the epilepsy. I came off the drug Phenytoin and felt like I had joined the human race for the first time. I met a woman in London, Francesca, who didn't take any of my shit. We're still together and happily married and have two wonderful children. Who would have thought.

I got a new job at Sky TV and they gave me the money to make my first movie as a producer: *Tube Tales*. I loved the experience. Life was working for the first time. The anxiety was history and the mood swings were under control. I came out of a screening of my film one morning at a Soho preview cinema and I had over 100 missed calls from numbers I didn't recognise. Something was up.

The news that Stuart Adamson had taken his own life was a shock. I hadn't seen him in a while and had no idea he had been struggling with an alcohol problem. Our paths had crossed a few times and I had even interviewed him on my TV show. We got along fine. No acrimony, no bitterness, no envy. He was still a friend, distant but someone I respected and cared about. It's strange everyone always thought it would be me that took his own life. The period when we were working on *The Absolute Game* was close. But not Stuart. I never saw that coming.

I hosted his memorial service in Dunfermline at the Carnegie Hall which was an emotional evening. He was clearly loved by many, many people. I've been told stories of what he did to me behind my back, really awful personal stuff. I don't want to remember him for that: I want to remember his big smile. His amazing talent. The way we

Into The Valley

passed each other in mid-air during a live gig —young and free.

My brother Michael who is still in the music business encouraged me to celebrate the bands 30th anniversary by playing T in the Park, an open air festival in Scotland. What a day. Standing alongside Bruce and Jamie Watson, Bill Simpson and Mike Bailley was a moment to cherish. 60,000 people singing along with 'Into the Valley' and the now better known 'The Saints are Coming', thanks to the cool cover version done by U2 and Green Day.

When it came to doing a 40th Anniversary our friends in England, Ireland and Wales asked why we never played further afield than Scotland. It was impossible to get tickets for these one-off events.

Was it possible that we could do a few more gigs? Would anyone be interested? I had my doubts. Bruce and Jamie have a day job with Big Country but we decided collectively to work around their busy schedules and try to wander around the UK, and hopefully people might turn up (they did and it has been amazing).

I met my friend Martin Glover aka Youth, producer to the stars and member of Killing Joke at the funeral of our dear friend Jazz Summers. An inspiration to both of us and much missed every day. Youth had heard that we might be doing a few dates. I told him about my fears that the band were headed into the nostalgia heritage trail and that I wasn't comfortable with that. He told me that he had always been a big Skids fan and we should write some new music together in the style of The Skids.

What? What? What? What? What? What?

He suggested that I come down to his house and studio in South London and try a few things out. I reminded him that I hadn't been near that environment since the last days

Into The Valley

of The Armoury Show. He tried to convince me with an, if it's in you it never leaves you speech. I'm not sure I was ready to buy-in to this idea but he's a very persuasive person and wouldn't listen to any doubts or negative stuff. It was on — we were going to give it a go. If it didn't work then so what.

I arrived at Youths studio with a few scraps of paper with a few rough ideas and lyrics. He played me a backing track he had written in the Skids style. It was full of energy and had a melodic edge. It sounded like the Skids that I had once loved. There was a ghost in the room but the ghost felt part of the modern world.

He left me there on my own with the backing track and I started to try and make some of my ideas fit. I had been working on a new movie project with my friend Hamish McAlpine about the early years of the romance between Ian Brady and Myra Hindley. It is called Saddleworth and is set on the moors. I felt that if nothing else happened I might get an edit credit song for the film.

Youth listened to the words and hated them. He reminded me that the Skids were a positive force and these lyrics were entirely negative and poisonous. Of course he told me this in his nice hippy-punk way but he made it clear the verses were terrible. He loved the idea of the moors and wanted me to not lose that idea. No one has ever done that to me before, pulled my words apart. He was right. Within an hour I had completely reshaped the songs meaning and now it was an anthem about escaping city life and looking for nature to release a sense of freedom. It worked. The edge was there. The melody was very Skids. The chorus was magic.

In this mad house where on one day he was working with me in one room, Nik Turner from Hawkwind in another, a Norwegian thrash metal band upstairs and a bunch of sufi-mystics doing Killing Joke covers in the basement just about captures the madness.

The song we worked was called 'Up On The Moors'. The first new Skids song in 35 years. The music felt relevant. Exactly what we needed, to get off the nostalgia trail. It was the beginning of a new chapter, full of fury and energy without ever becoming a cliché. I played it to the rest of the band and they loved it. Everyone wanted to be part of something new. Suddenly we were recording. Youth was mixing and very quickly we had *Burning Cities*. It was recorded like the old days. Fast. No fucking about. No pompous production — just hard and simple and full of passion.

I could feel the ghost of Stuart Adamson smiling as we recorded the songs. The lyrics, then the vocals came fast. It was how we used to love working.

Youth turned the recording into a magical experience for all of us. Whatever it is — he has it. Alchemy? Magic? Love of Music? Maybe all of those things. We toured in 2017 and even managed to sell out The Roundhouse. Bloody Hell. We now play the new songs from *Burning Cities*, an album that went into the UK top twenty. The world's insane and we as a band are reflecting that. Every gig is given care love and attention. We are proud of what we have achieved. And most importantly we care about our audience. Who knows what will happen next.

Into The Valley

INTO THE VALLEY

I took the title from one of my favourite school poems: *The Charge of The Light Brigade* by Tennyson. The words have often been misinterpreted and misunderstood.

I've been offered on many occasions to go TV shows so they can have a laugh at the songs expense as they try to decipher what I'm on about. Fuck them.

The song is about something serious and without being pompous I'm proud of the words and don't feel the modern day need to do anything for publicity and mock my own work, something I wrote when I was 16.

The song means as much to me today as it did then. This was the song that broke the Skids from being a cult band to taking our music to a much wider audience. This is the song that people remember and when we play it live and it's clear that people know by heart the very words that seem ripe for misinterpretation.

I love Bill Simpson's bass and Stuart Adamson's iconic guitar line. It's not my favourite Skids song but the memory of those long days in the Carnegie library in Dunfermline where I wrote it and many other Skids lyrics remains with me to this day. I loved the silence of the library and the different types of people who came in and out throughout the day. It was a magical space that offered me a sanctuary

Into The Valley

to write and I was never asked what I was doing or that I should leave. I was left to get on with creating these mini-narratives.

In simple terms 'Into the Valley' is an anti-war song. As mentioned in the story, it was originally titled 'Depersonalised', which probably gives more of a flavour of what the content is all about. Our producer David Bachelor thought it wasn't the catchiest of titles and gently coerced me to change it to 'Into the Valley'.

The second line 'Betrothed and Divine' is about how people become wedded to causes and ideologies. In the case of soldiers, indoctrinated to do a job. This has caused some of the most destructive periods in our shared history: The Nazis, Stalin, and more recently Isis.

This disease is catching from victory to stone.

This alludes to military indoctrination as a disease, where the end result is always the same: death, slaughter, a tombstone. A visit to the memorials of WW1 in Northern France and Belgium is always a humbling experience. When you see the ages of the young men who died on either side of the conflict you realise the futility and nihilism of war. Names carved on stone so we can remember never to do this again, until the next time.

Ahoy! Ahoy!

The chorus starts like a celebration of the world around us: the land, the sea and the sky.

It moved though through the evolution of a young man and then fatally explains that so many are deceased or fatally wounded, finishing with the ironic line 'Long May they die.'

The idea at play being that this useless loss of life will never end.

The second verse begins with the horror of what it might have been like to be suddenly vulnerable and helpless. The words attack the system that perpetuates this:

Why so uncertain this culture deceives, prophesied, brainwashed, tomorrows demise.
All systems failing the placards unroll.

This could be about today. The way we are deceived and lied to and how our systems that are meant to protect us have failed us. Trump, Brexit, Putin…terrifying stuff. We used the song recently with two young girls singing it as a lament as the dead British soldiers from the recent Iraq conflict were scrolled on a Video screen. It can still be seen on YouTube.

The final verse was meant to give a sense of order. It's time that we gathered our thoughts and pushed for answers.

A collector's dilemma repositioned and filed.

This line seems to have caused much confusion or mystery amongst Skids fans. I've never tried to explain it before, preferring people to find their own meanings, but here goes:

The first part refers to media moguls, warmongers and politicians who create these tragedies. They treat these tragedies as great moments in their lives, a collection of great honours. I was trying to say that they might have to think again as history will eventually shine a different light on their propaganda and decision making and put it another box - war criminals.

Into The Valley